THE
TRAVEL
QUIZ
BOOK

PUZZLES, BRAIN TEASERS AND
TRIVIA QUESTIONS FOR
PEOPLE WHO LOVE TRAVEL

DANIEL AUSTIN

BradtGUIDES

First edition published October 2020
Bradt Travel Guides Ltd
31a High Street, Chesham, Buckinghamshire, HP5 1BW, England
www.bradtguides.com
Print edition published in the USA by The Globe Pequot Press Inc,
PO Box 480, Guilford, Connecticut 06437-0480

ISBN: 978 1 78477 794 4

British Library Cataloguing in Publication Data
A catalogue record for this book is available from the British Library

Photograph, illustration and map credits (page references in parentheses):
Alex Tai/ Noun Project (34); Anna Laura Bussi/Noun Project (34); Anniken & Andreas/
Noun Project (34); Barrasa8 (14); Charl Durand/Unsplash (15); Colin Capelle (14);
Dan Merino (15); DinosoftLab/Noun Project (34); Flatart/Freepik (168, 169); Francisco
Antunes (14); Francisco Anzola (160); FreeVectorMaps.com (9, 23, 30, 31, 53, 61,
73, 81, 88, 93, 99, 106, 122, 127, 143, 150, 176, 190); Golan Levin (14); Hadi/Noun
Project (113); Hans Johnson (160); Hash Milhan (161); Henry Ryder/Noun Project
(72); ibrandify/Freepik (34, 80, 81); Justin Vidamo (161); LukeL/Pixabay (161); Michaela
Loheit (160); Nikita Kozin/Noun Project (34); Norbert Aepli (15); Paul Keller (15);
SmashingMag/Freepik (8, 60, 61, 112, 113); Werner Bayer (160); Yu-Chan Chen
(161). All trademarks are property of their respective owners (38, 39, 180, 181).

Typeset by Ian Spick, Bradt Travel Guides
Production managed by Jellyfish Print Solutions; printed in the UK

CONTENTS

INTRODUCTION

As this book goes to print, the world of travel has been unexpectedly turned on its head by the pandemic – with lockdown triggering pangs of wanderlust in travel lovers the world over. And so it is a curiously apt moment, as everyone dreams of their next getaway, to reflect on what many of us may be guilty of having taken for granted. The opportunity to travel is a valuable one, at once enriching, mind-broadening and a welcome antidote to the drudgeries of daily life.

Intrepid globetrotters and armchair travellers alike will, I trust, find a little of the magic of travel captured in the 2,200 themed questions and puzzles between the covers of this book. I have endeavoured to make it more than just a quiz book with which to test your worldly knowledge: each section has been crafted so that, whether or not you know the answers, you will learn something new. It will be just the ticket for travel fanatics whether you're looking to improve your knowledge of the world, planning a quiz night for family and friends, or just want to while away the hours of a long-haul flight. My earnest hope is that on occasions – curiosity piqued – you will feel compelled to cast this book aside and reach for an atlas, encyclopaedia or Google in a quest to discover more on a particular topic.

I have been captivated by trivia, brain teasers and puzzles for as long as I can remember, but my 'day job' as a travel author is writing about my specialist area of Madagascar (including multiple guides published by Bradt). Despite this particular passion, you will be pleased to hear that I have succeeded in exercising great self-restraint, limiting myself to no more than a dozen questions on this extraordinary island nation! My aim has been to make the quizzes as diverse as possible, including plenty of unusual destinations alongside those that are more familiar. This is very much in the spirit of Bradt Travel Guides, which has a long history of publishing pioneering guides to places that fall below the usual tourist radar.

My thanks are due to all the various experts in specific destinations, cultures and languages who have kindly double-checked the accuracy of questions and answers falling outside the realm of my own expertise. Above all, I am indebted to fellow travel writer and former ace puzzle-setter Janice Booth, who not only took time out from putting the finishing touches to her own Bradt guide to Socotra to cast her eye over this entire book, but also contributed the fiendish logic grid on page 188.

QUESTIONS
&
PUZZLES

1 EAST IS EAST
Answers on page 198

1. Who was the founder and first emperor of the Mongol Empire in 1206?

2. Which of these is not one of the 12 animals of the traditional Chinese zodiac? Dog, dragon, horse, lion, rabbit, rat.

3. The hereditary military nobility and officer caste known as the Samurai originated in medieval times in which country?

4. In which century was the Taj Mahal built?

5. The 2012 viral dance craze known as Gangnam Style takes its name from a district of which capital city?

6. The Dayak are any of several dozen groups of native tribespeople living on which island?

7. Just 64km (40 miles) wide at its narrowest point, the Palk Strait separates which island from the Asian continental mainland?

8. Located in an area of central Cambodia designated as a UNESCO Biosphere Reserve, what kind of geographical feature is Tonlé Sap?

9. Which of the following is *not* a variety of Asian noodles? Misua, ramen, soba, sōmen, udon, yakitori.

10. Which number is considered unlucky in Chinese superstition because it sounds similar to the word for 'death'?

11. Which river provides the main water supply for Ho Chi Minh City?

12. The Kumbh Mela festival, involving a pilgrimage and ritual dip in the Ganges, Godavari or Shipra, is celebrated by followers of which religion?

13. What is the capital city of Bangladesh?

14. Hangul is a phonetic alphabet system created in 1443 and used for writing which Asian language with over 70 million native speakers?

15. Which of these martial arts did *not* originate in Japan? Aikido, judo, jujutsu, sumo, tai chi, taidō.

2 FOOD FOR THOUGHT
Answers on page 198

Match each trio of traditional foods listed below to the country with which they are closely associated.

1.	enchiladas, fajitas, guacamole	Belgium
2.	souvlaki, spanakopita, taramasalata	Brazil
3.	miso soup, sashimi, tempura	China
4.	cinnamon bun, gravlax, toast Skagen	Colombia
5.	brigadeiros, feijoada, pão de queijo	Ethiopia
6.	chow mein, mantou, wonton soup	Greece
7.	biltong, bunny chow, malva pudding	Hungary
8.	green curry, pad phak, tom yum	Iran
9.	corn dog, hamburger, hominy grits	Italy
10.	carbonade flamande, mussels and fries, waffles	Jamaica
11.	lasagne, risotto, tiramisu	Japan
12.	bibimbap, hotteok, kimchi	Mexico
13.	fisherman's soup, goulash, lángos	South Africa
14.	bangers and mash, spotted dick, toad in the hole	South Korea
15.	raclette, rösti, tartiflette	Spain
16.	bandeja paisa, chocolate con queso, pandebono	Sweden
17.	ackee and saltfish, escoveitch fish, jerk chicken	Switzerland
18.	injera, kitfo, tibs	Thailand
19.	chorizo, gazpacho soup, paella	United Kingdom
20.	abgoosht/dizi, gheimeh, ghormeh sabzi	USA

3 REBRANDING
Answers on page 198

This quiz is about places that used to be known by a different name in the past.

1. Tea aficionados will be familiar with 'Ceylon' as a variety of tea, but the country from which it originates has not been known by that name since 1972. What is it called now?

2. Constantinople was a major regional capital of the Roman Empire, but by what name is the city better known today?

3. In 1989, to what did Burma's military government change the country's name?

4. Immortalised in the title of a 1989 West End hit musical, what was the name of Vietnam's most populous city before it became Ho Chi Minh City?

5. The king of Swaziland changed the official name of his country in 2018 to mark fifty years of independence, a move partly motivated by frequent confusion with Switzerland. What is it called now?

6. Prior to 1995, India's financial capital of Mumbai was known by what other six-letter word that lives on in the name of a spicy snack comprising a variety of dried ingredients?

7. The west African nation of Burkina Faso was a French colony until 1960, but what two-word name was it known by at that time?

8. The city of Leningrad was previously called Petrograd, but how has it been known since 1991?

9. From the 1970s to the 1990s, the Democratic Republic of the Congo was known by what five-letter name, derived from a local word meaning 'river'?

10. The capital city of Kazakhstan has had many names: founded less than a century ago as Akmoly, it later became Akmolinsk, then Tselinograd, then Akmola, then Astana, but in 2019 it was changed again to honour the country's outgoing president. What is it called now?

11. Zimbabwe is named after one of its most ancient cities, but the country's previous name honoured a now-controversial British colonial founder. Who?

12. New York City is so called because it was captured in a 1664 mission organised by the Duke of York. What was its name up to that point?

13. Which country was briefly known as the Khmer Republic in the 1970s, then as Kampuchea until 1989?

14. The town of Speed was renamed SpeedKills for one month in 2011 as part of a road safety awareness campaign. Where is Speed?

15. The present-day capital city of which country was called Edo (sometimes written as Jedo or Yedo) before becoming the capital in 1868?

16. Siamese twins, Siamese cats and Siamese fighting fish all take their name from Siam, but by what name has that country been known since the 1940s?

17. What name, synonymous with hot curries, was how the Indian city of Chennai was known until 1996?

18. The capital of Zimbabwe used to share its name with an English cathedral city not far from Stonehenge. What was Harare called before being renamed in 1982?

19. Which Australian state was known until the mid-19th century as Van Diemen's Land, in honour of Dutch colonial governor Anthony van Diemen?

20. The name 'Peking' was a spelling created by early French missionaries. How is the name of this Chinese city usually transcribed in English nowadays?

4 STREETS AHEAD
Answers on page 198

1. The Champs-Élysées in Paris runs from Place de la Concorde to which famous landmark?

2. Which New York City thoroughfare is home to the world's two largest stock exchanges?

3. What is the name of Barcelona's famous pedestrianised avenue with the Columbus Monument at its lower end?

4. Meaning literally 'rice mill', what is the name of the short street in central Bangkok that has become a hub for backpackers travelling in Asia?

5. What is the name of the processional route through Jerusalem's old city, believed to be the path that Jesus walked on the way to his crucifixion?

6. Which short London street once had 20 townhouses and a pub called the Rose and Crown, but has been blocked off to public access since the 1970s despite legally still being a public right of way?

7. A succession of several streets forms the main thoroughfare through Edinburgh's historic centre. By what two-word name is it popularly known?

8. The elegant pedestrianised street known as Istiklal Avenue leads to the main square of which large city?

9. Officially called Placa, what is the more common name of the main street through the historic centre of Dubrovnik in Croatia?

10. Lombard Street is famed for a steep section with no fewer than eight tight bends. In which US city is it located?

11. In which country would you find streets called No Name Lane, Tiddy Widdy Beach Road, Titwobble Lane, Cat Jump Road, and Bionic Ear Lane?

12. Orchard Road – named for the fruit and spice plantations it once led to – is a famous shopping street and tourist attraction in which Asian capital city?

5 CHART TOPPER
Answers on page 198

Can you match each city with the corresponding climate chart, showing its monthly precipitation (grey bars) and daytime temperature (black lines)?

1. Brisbane, Australia

4. London, United Kingdom

2. Cape Town, South Africa

5. São Paulo, Brazil

3. Istanbul, Turkey

6. Tokyo, Japan

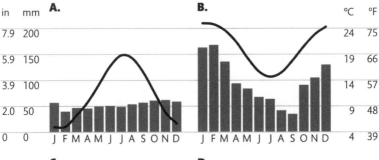

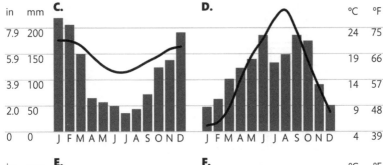

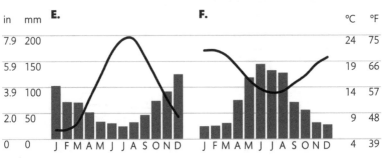

6 LANDMARKS OF THE NEW WORLD
Answers on page 198

Identify the famous sights depicted below and connect each one to its correct location on the map.

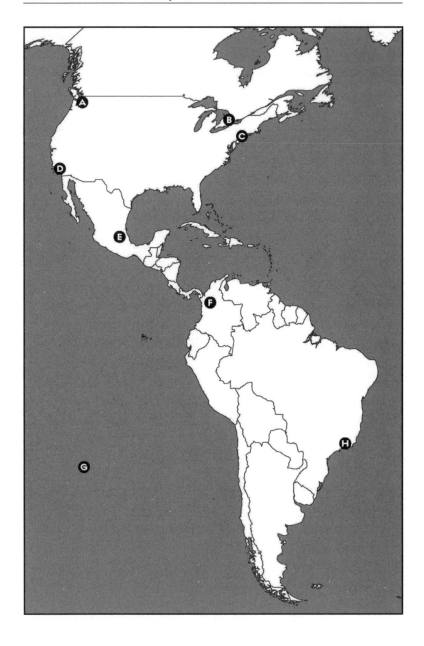

7 THE SEVEN SEAS (AND A DOZEN MORE)
Answers on page 198

In the grid below, find 19 seas and oceans of the world. Words may run forwards or backwards in a vertical, horizontal or diagonal direction.

S	O	U	T	H	C	H	I	N	A
O	T	A	S	M	A	N	L	R	L
L	A	N	J	A	V	A	A	I	A
O	C	A	E	C	B	B	B	R	R
M	C	M	N	R	I	Y	L	I	A
O	U	A	A	A	A	T	A	S	N
N	L	D	N	N	E	B	C	H	A
I	O	N	I	A	N	G	K	R	P
R	M	A	G	N	I	R	E	B	A
E	N	I	T	N	E	G	R	A	J

8 PETER PIPER'S PICKLED PEPPERS
Answers on page 198

The answers to all of these general knowledge questions begin with 'P'.

1. What is the name of the junction that marks the southern end of London's Regent Street, known for its large video display screens?

2. What is the name of the ruined temple on the Athenian Acropolis?

3. What is the capital and largest city of the de facto independent state of Kosovo?

4. Which country produces more than half of the world's supply of cork?

5. What is the name for the scaly mammals of Africa and Asia that subsist mainly on a diet of ants and termites?

6. What body of water is separated from the Gulf of Oman by the Strait of Hormuz?

7. What is the name of the twin-towered skyscraper in Kuala Lumpur that was the world's tallest building from 1998 to 2004?

8. The Astronomical Clock is mounted on the wall of the Old Town Hall in the Old Town Square of which European capital?

9. Which capital city is built on the banks of the Taedong River?

10. The guaraní is the unit of currency used in which country?

11. What is the name for the large peninsula of southern Greece connected to the mainland by the Isthmus of Corinth?

12. Which southern Italian city is the capital of the autonomous region of Sicily?

13. Which is the only member of the bear family that is completely vegetarian?

14. Which Asian capital city's ceremonial name is Krong Chaktomuk?

15. Which unincorporated territory of the United States is located in the Caribbean, just west of the British Virgin Islands?

9 BRADT TRAVEL GUIDES
Answers on page 198

The initial letters of each answer to the questions in this general knowledge quiz spell out the name BRADT TRAVEL GUIDES.

1. What B is an Italian luxury brand – known for its jewellery, watches, fragrances and leather products – which, with the addition of one letter to the end, becomes the name of a European country?

2. What R is a 2007 Disney-Pixar animated movie set in Paris that shares its name with a traditional French Provençal stewed vegetable dish, typically made with ingredients that include tomatoes, onions, courgettes and aubergines?

3. What A is a coastal Moroccan city referenced in the title of a 1977 song by Mike Batt, which was covered by Boney M four years later? It is the largest seaside resort in the country, with excellent beaches and an unusually mild climate year-round.

4. What D is the two-word title given to the foremost spiritual leader of the Gelug school of Tibetan Buddhism? Over more than six centuries, a total of 14 people have held this title.

5. What T became an Olympic sport in 2000 and is the national sport of South Korea? Its origins date back to the years immediately following World War II, and the first official governing body was set up in 1959.

6. What T is the southernmost island country in the Caribbean, located just 11km (7 miles) off the coast of Venezuela? It is known for its fossil-fuel wealth and has the third-highest GDP per capita in the Americas after the USA and Canada.

7. What R is an omnivorous and nocturnal North American animal, closely related to kinkajous, olingos and olinguitos? The creature has also become established as an invasive species in several parts of Europe, most notably Germany, as well as in Japan.

8. What A is the UNESCO World Heritage Site with a famous entrance gate that bears the slogan 'arbeit macht frei'? Around 2 million tourists visit the site each year.

9. What V is the city where you would find the Pio-Clementino Museum housing Greek and Roman sculptures, the Gregorian Egyptian Museum, the Chiaramonti Museum with over a thousand antique statues, the Anima Mundi Ethnological Museum of world cultures, and the Profane Museum of miscellaneous artifacts?

10. What E is the proper name of the clock tower of the Houses of Parliament in London, which contains the great bell of Big Ben?

11. What L is the modern city where you would find the ruins of the city of Thebes, known to the ancient Egyptians as Waset? Nowadays, the area is frequently characterised as the 'world's greatest open-air museum'.

12. What G is the surname of an African leader who died at the hands of an angry mob in 2011? As a newly graduated army recruit some 45 years previously, he had spent nine months on an English-language course in the Buckinghamshire village of Beaconsfield in the United Kingdom.

13. What U is an Indo-Aryan language also known as Lashkari, with approximately 70 million native speakers (and an even greater number of second-language speakers) across the Indian subcontinent?

14. What I is the first name of Prime Minister Khan of Pakistan, who was elected to this office in 2018?

15. What D is a country that comprises the majority of the peninsula of Jutland – known in ancient times as the Cimbrian Peninsula – along with more than 400 islands?

16. What E is a two-word euphemistic phrase, widely popularised by the media during the Bosnian War of the 1990s, that refers to the ruthless removal or genocide of one particular racial or religious group by the forces of another?

17. What S is a Japanese drink – known locally as 'nihonshu' or 'seishu' – that is made by fermenting rice that has been polished? It is often served with some ceremony, gently warmed in an earthenware bottle then sipped from a small porcelain cup called a sakazuki.

10 PICTURE POSTCARD
Answers on page 199

1. What is the name of this astonishing collection of sculptures, that were inscribed as a UNESCO World Heritage in 1987?

2. This small but famous sculpture (a replica of the 400-year-old original, which is kept in a nearby museum) can be found in which city?

3. In which country is the Cave of Hands, pictured here?

4. The Chocolate Hills are – somewhat disappointingly – actually made of limestone. In which country would you find them?

5. What is the name of this iconic site, voted one of the 'New Seven Wonders of the World' in 2007?

6. Situated on a hill overlooking which capital city would you find the place shown here?

7. What is the name of this gigantic ravine in southern Namibia?

8. In which city is this famous bridge located and what is it called?

11 A RISING STAR
Answers on page 199

Match each of the nations – plus the EU – listed below with the number of stars that feature on its official flag. (We are only talking about geometric stars here, rather than the astronomical definition, so representations of the Sun don't count!)

1.	Australia	no stars
2.	Bangladesh	1 star
3.	Brazil	2 stars
4.	Cape Verde	3 stars
5.	China	4 stars
6.	Cook Islands	5 stars
7.	European Union	6 stars
8.	Grenada	7 stars
9.	New Zealand	8 stars
10.	Philippines	9 stars
11.	Syria	10 stars
12.	Turkey	12 stars
13.	Tuvalu	15 stars
14.	USA	27 stars
15.	Venezuela	50 stars

12 FOLLOWED TO THE LETTER
Answers on page 199

1. Which tiny European country is an anagram of 'ROMANIANS'?

2. Find five countries with four-letter names. (If you find that too easy, can you think of five more?)

3. The name of which South American country includes *none* of the first three letters of the alphabet?

4. The name of which South American country includes *all* of the first three letters of the alphabet?

5. The 11-letter name of which country contains no letter more than once?

6. Which African nation is an anagram of 'CHEESYSELL'?

7. The letters of 'Iran' and 'Benin' alternate between vowels and consonants. What's the longest country name you can find with this property?

8. Five European capital cities begin with V; which is the northernmost?

9. The name of which African country contains all five vowels – A, E, I, O and U – exactly once?

10. The name of which European country contains none of the same letters that appear in 'HOLIDAY'?

11. Which remote island nation is an anagram of 'ACRIMONIES'?

12. Which country name is the odd one out and why? Bahamas, Ghana, Kazakhstan, Madagascar, Morocco, Panama, Rwanda.

13. Berlin and Brussels are two European capitals beginning with B. Can you name five more?

14. Which is the only country in the world whose name is typed using only letters from a single row of a QWERTY keyboard?

15. Which country's name is an anagram of the first six letters of a day of the week?

13 NIGHT AT THE MUSEUM
Answers on page 199

1. Which country is home to museums separately dedicated to pencils, lawnmowers, and dog collars?

2. The Phallological Museum is to be found in the capital city of which country?

3. The Museum of Vampires and Legendary Creatures opened in 1986 in the building of a former train station in which capital city?

4. In which country would you find the International Museum of Toilets?

5. Which country is home to museums separately dedicated to salt and pepper shakers, celebrity lingerie, and clowns?

6. Which city – the world's lowest-lying capital – is home to the Museum of Miniature Books as well as a carpet museum? It also hosted the Eurovision Song Contest in 2012.

7. Edvard Munch produced four versions of his famous painting *The Scream*. One was sold to a private collector in 2012; in which European city would you find the other three?

8. Four of the world's top ten most-visited museums are in which city?

9. In which country did a pair of former lovers join forces to set up the Museum of Broken Relationships in 2006? The museum's collection toured the world before settling in its permanent home in 2010, going on to inspire both a spin-off museum in Los Angeles and the Swedish Museum of Failure.

10. In which country would you find Froggyland, a museum exhibiting more than 500 stuffed frogs arranged in a series of humorous humanlike scenes? The amphibians were preserved by taxidermist Ferenc Mere in the 1910s.

11. Which art gallery is the world's most-visited museum?

12. Which country is home to museums separately dedicated to sand, bonsai and instant noodles?

13. Opened in 1683, the first university museum in England – and, some argue, the first public museum in the world – was located in Oxford. It moved to a new building in the 1840s but is still operating to this day. What is it called?

14. The world's only Cornish pasty museum is located more than 8,000km (5,000 miles) from Cornwall, in which country? Each year since 2009, the town where the museum is located has held an International Pasty Festival.

15. At which museum in Washington DC can you see the Apollo 11 command module *Columbia*?

16. Which famous London museum is located opposite the Natural History Museum and Science Museum?

17. In which European city would you find at least three museums dedicated to architect Antoni Gaudí?

18. Which city is home to museums separately dedicated to trains, chocolate and comic strips?

19. In which city would you find a seven-storey museum dedicated to a single brand of beer? It opened in 2000 and by 2019 had welcomed 20 million visitors through its doors.

20. The most-visited art gallery in the United States is in New York City. What is it called?

14 JULES VERNE ADVENTURE

Answers on page 199

Across

7. Capital of Switzerland (4)

8. Easiest way to access top of Cape Town's Table Mountain (5,3)

9. UK's southernmost national park (8)

10. Japanese alcoholic beverage made by fermenting rice (4)

11. Scandinavian toast or greeting (4)

12. *See 15 down*

14. Nationality of people from Honolulu (8)

16. Elephant's protruding tooth (4)

18. Protagonist of *15 down* (4)

20. Multi-leg flight (8)

22. *See 15 down*

23. Breathing hole made in ice by a seal (4)

Down

1. Largest city in New Jersey (6)

2. Asia Minor (8)

3. UN agency responsible for global air transportation (4)

4. City on Scotland's east coast, nicknamed 'Granite City' (8)

5. Scottish loch said to be inhabited by a monster (4)

6. World's deepest lake (6)

12. Periods before sunrise and after sunset (8)

13. Sudden flare-up of disease or disorder (8)

15 down, 12 across, 22 across & 21 down. Famous travel adventure by Jules Verne (6,3,5,2,6,4)

17. Largest island in the Mediterranean (6)

19. Coordinate system of a map (4)

21. *See 15 down*

15 FOUNTAINS OF FIRE
Answers on page 199

1. Which Italian volcano erupted in AD79, famously destroying several cities, including Pompeii and Herculaneum?

2. Three-quarters of the world's active and dormant volcanoes sit around the edge of the Pacific Ocean in a horseshoe-shaped line known as what?

3. Which famous volcanic feature in Northern Ireland was declared a UNESCO World Heritage Site in 1986?

4. In which country is Eyjafjallajökull, whose 2010 eruption led to the largest air-traffic shutdown since World War II, with some 30 countries affected and more than 100,000 flights cancelled?

5. Measured from its base on the sea bed, the world's tallest volcano is 10,200m (33,500 ft). As more than half of it is below sea level, its peak is 4,207m (13,803 ft) high. What is it called?

6. Ojos del Salado holds the title for the active volcano with the highest peak, reaching 6,893m (22,615 ft). In which mountain range is it located?

7. In 2019, which volcanic island in New Zealand's northeastern Bay of Plenty region erupted explosively with deadly consequences?

8. The 3,350m (11,000 ft) volcanic Mount Etna – also known locally as Mungibeddu – is found on which island?

9. What short word of Hawaiian origin – particularly familiar to Scrabble fanatics – means basaltic lava that is rough and jagged?

10. An eruption in which volcanic island group caused a deadly tsunami in Java and Sumatra in December 2018?

11. Kazumura in Hawaii is the largest known example in the world of what kind of volcanic feature, measuring 65km (41 miles)?

12. In 1982, all four engines of a jumbo jet shut down after it flew through a cloud of volcanic ash. The plane was able to land safely 180km (110 miles) away in Jakarta. Which airline was the flight operated by?

16 WATER, WATER EVERYWHERE
Answers on page 199

Match each of these bodies of water with the corresponding locations marked A–N on the map of Europe and the Middle East below.

1. Adriatic Sea

2. Alboran Sea

3. Bay of Biscay

4. Black Sea

5. Caspian Sea

6. Gulf of Aden

7. Gulf of Bothnia

8. Gulf of Sidra

9. Ionian Sea

10. Levantine Sea

11. Red Sea

12. Sea of Azov

13. Sea of Marmara

14. Tyrrhenian Sea

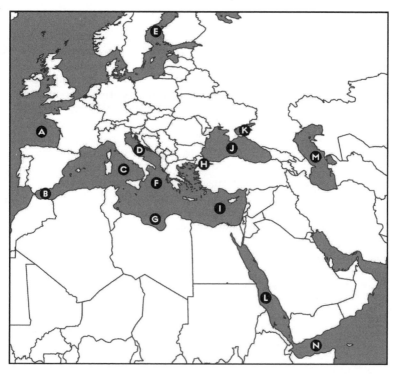

17 LIFE DOWN UNDER
Answers on page 199

In this quiz, see how much you know about Australia and New Zealand.

1. What is the name of the sea in which the Great Barrier Reef is located?

2. What is the largest city in New Zealand, with a population more than three times that of the capital?

3. Known locally as a yidaki or mago, what Australian Aboriginal wind instrument requires the player to master the technique of breathing in through the nose while simultaneously expelling air from the mouth?

4. What is the name of the Maori ritual famously performed by New Zealand's All Blacks rugby team before their matches?

5. Endemic to eastern Australia, the koala is an arboreal marsupial whose diet consists primarily of what?

6. Which of the following movies was not shot in New Zealand? *Lord of the Rings* trilogy (2001–2003); *The Last Samurai* (2003); *The Lion, The Witch and The Wardrobe* (2005); *Where the Wild Things Are* (2009).

7. Listed as an Australian National Heritage since 2011, what is the name of the famous 243km (151-mile) stretch of the B100 road in southeast Australia that provides access to the coastal limestone formations known as the Twelve Apostles?

8. How many hours ahead of GMT is New Zealand's time zone?

9. What is the capital city of Australia?

10. Which of these cities in New Zealand is *not* located on North Island? Auckland, Christchurch, Hamilton, Tauranga, Wellington.

11. In Australian slang, what is a 'bottle-o'?

12. New Zealand takes its name from Zeeland, the least populous province of which country?

13. What is Australia's national gemstone? The majority of the global supply of this gem comes from there.

14. What is the meaning of the Maori word 'Aotearoa'?

15. Which of these Australian animals is not a member of the kangaroo family? Pademelon, possum, quokka, tree-kangaroo, wallaby, wallaroo.

16. What is the name of the sea that separates Australia from New Zealand?

17. Several very large sculptures have been built as tourist traps along major routes in Australia since the 1960s. Which one of these is *not* real? Big Pineapple, Giant Koala, Big Prawn, Giant Caterpillar, Big Penguin.

18. In Wellington, New Zealand, what is nicknamed 'the Beehive'?

19. An Australian comedian caused a minor international diplomatic incident in 2006 by listing what for sale on eBay, with a starting price of 1 cent? The bidding reached A\$3,000 before the auction was pulled.

20. Which river, the longest in New Zealand, runs through the city of Hamilton?

21. Australian Howard Florey shared the Nobel Prize in Physiology or Medicine in 1945 for his role in the discovery and development of what?

22. What was the name of New Zealand's first female prime minister?

23. What is Australia's largest desert called?

24. New Zealand's national day, 6 February, marks the anniversary of the signing of a treaty between the British Crown and Maori chiefs in 1840. What is the name of this treaty and also of the associated public holiday?

25. In Mbabaram, an Australian Aboriginal language of north Queensland that became extinct in 1979 with the death of its last remaining speaker, what is surprising about the word for dog?

18 UNCONVENTIONAL SAFARIS
Answers on page 200

Five crackpot friends are planning separate trips to different destinations across Africa in search of their favourite animals, taking some frankly improbable modes of transport. Using the clues below, can you figure out who's going where, how and with what objective?

Complete the table with these details. You may find it helpful to use the logic grid for assistance (by marking positive and negative relationships with ticks and crosses respectively). Each option in each category appears exactly once in the solution.

1. The person hoping to see elephants won't be travelling by hovercraft.

2. Of the trip undertaken by Emil and the visit to Tanzania, one will focus on leopards and the other will involve a great deal of exhausting bouncing on a pogo stick.

3. In an alphabetical list of the five travellers' names, the person whose dream is to go on donkeyback appears before the fan of buffalos.

4. Emil has his sights set on a safari to Zambia.

5. Botswana is the place where lions will be sought.

6. In the alphabetical list of names, the person travelling to Gabon appears immediately after the one whose dream is to see a buffalo.

7. The purpose of the devil-may-care penny-farthing adventure is to find a pride of wild lions.

8. Rhinos are the number one species Bertie is excited to see on his trip.

		Country					Transport					Animal				
		Botswana	Gabon	Kenya	Tanzania	Zambia	Donkey riding	Hovercraft	Penny-farthing	Pogo stick	Sedan chair	Buffalo	Elephant	Leopard	Lion	Rhino
Name	Angela															
	Bertie																
	Carmen																
	Darcelle																
	Emil																
Animal	Buffalo																
	Elephant																
	Leopard																
	Lion																
	Rhino																
Transport	Donkey riding																
	Hovercraft																
	Penny-farthing																	
	Pogo stick																	
	Sedan chair																	

Name	Country	Transport	Animal
Angela			
Bertie			
Carmen			
Darcelle			
Emil			

19 SHE SELLS SEA SHELLS
Answers on page 200

The answers to all of these general knowledge questions begin with 'S'.

1. What word is typically used to refer to Denmark, Norway and Sweden collectively?

2. In which country would you find the islands of Praslin, La Digue, Desroches and Silhouette, as well as the Aldabra and Cosmoledo atolls?

3. Ljubljana Castle overlooks the Ljubljanica River in which country?

4. Which Australian landmark, opened in 1932, was designed and built by Middlesbrough-based British firm Dorman Long?

5. What is the capital of Bulgaria?

6. In the 2016 film *La La Land*, Mia sings about her aunt who 'spent a month sneezing' after falling into which river whose 'water was freezing'?

7. What is the name of the capital city of the US state of New Mexico?

8. Which Greek island is the remnant of a volcanic caldera, known for the whitewashed houses of its main towns, Fira and Oia?

9. Which city situated on Germany's Neckar River is home to the headquarters of Mercedes-Benz, Daimler and Porsche?

10. In which Canadian province are Regina, Prince Albert and Moose Jaw?

11. Being almost twice as tall as Tokyo Tower, which broadcasting and observation tower dominates the Japanese capital's skyline?

12. Music groups Alcazar, Roxette and Ace of Base are from which country?

13. Which city was the scene of the event that triggered World War I, namely the assassination of the Archduke Franz Ferdinand of Austria?

14. In which country would you find Dinder and Radom national parks?

15. Which capital city has in previous eras been known by the names Wiryeseong, Hanyang, Hanseong, Keijō and Gyeongseong?

20 MAKING A NAME FOR YOURSELF
Answers on page 200

Match these country names in English with the corresponding name in that country's own language:

1. Albania	Éire
2. Belgium	Deutschland
3. Croatia	Kalaallit Nunaat
4. Egypt	Shqipëria
5. Finland	Norge
6. Germany	Magyarország
7. Greece	Misr
8. Greenland	Hrvatska
9. Hungary	Hellas
10. Ireland	Belgique
11. Japan	Suomi
12. Norway	Nippon

21 TREASURE ISLAND
Answers on page 200

Can you identify each of the following islands from their outlines? (Note that the islands are not necessarily countries; they may be parts of countries or even contain territory of multiple countries.)

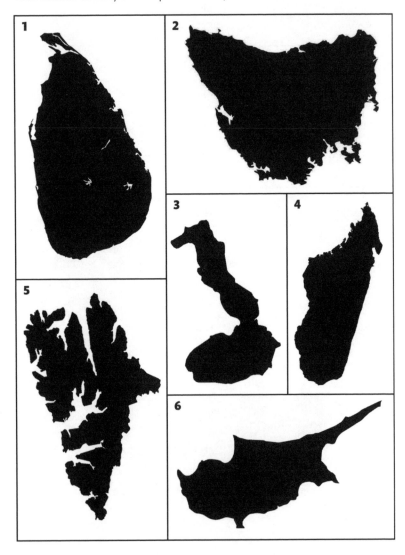

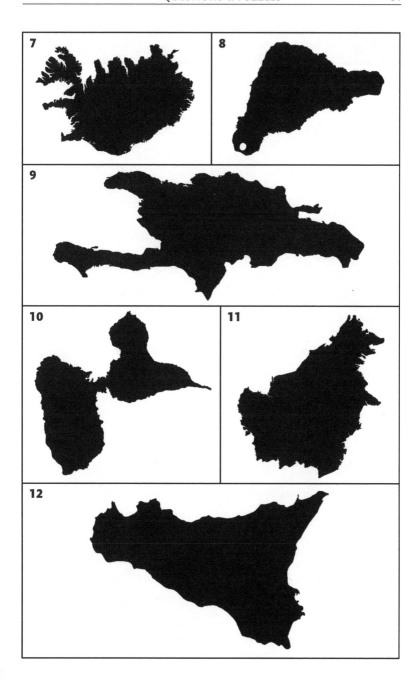

22 CITY LIGHTS
Answers on page 200

For each trio of cities listed, enter into the corresponding line of the grid the name of the country where you would find them.

When completed, the shaded boxes will spell out vertically a popular nickname of one of the cities listed in the clues.

1. Kraków, Lublin, Poznań

2. Giza, Luxor, Zagazig

3. Bremen, Bonn, Dortmund

4. Curitiba, Manaus, São Paulo

5. Eindhoven, The Hague, Utrecht

6. Agadir, Fez, Tangier

7. Metz, Rouen, Strasbourg

8. Dubrovnik, Rijeka, Split

9. Bloemfontein, East London, Port Elizabeth

10. Arequipa, Cusco, Puno

11. Faro, Lagos, Porto

12. Hyderabad, Lucknow, Pune

13. Basel, Lausanne, Lucerne

14. Beersheba, Nazareth, Safed

15. Babruysk, Grodno, Minsk

16. Antalya, Bodrum, İzmir

17. Aleppo, Homs, Latakia

18. Camagüey, Havana, Varadero

23 TUNNEL VISION
Answers on page 200

Identify each of these cities from their metro maps.

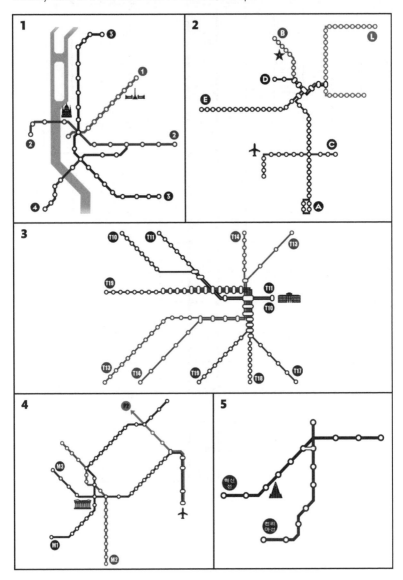

24 AT A LOSS FOR WORDS
Answers on page 200

1. In what language might someone alert you to their need for medical assistance with the words *j'ai besoin d'un médecin*?

2. You may be greeted with the words *Ciao! Che piacere vederti!* by a speaker of what language?

3. In which country would you find *heddlu* written on police cars?

4. The sentence *Esel essen Nesseln nicht, Nesseln essen Esel nicht* (donkeys don't eat nettles and nettles don't eat donkeys) is a tongue twister in which language?

5. Sticking with the donkey theme, in what language does the expression *alimentar um burro a pão-de-ló* (literally: feeding sponge cake to a donkey) mean to treat an undeserving person nicely?

6. What is the general word for 'cheese' in French?

7. In what small island nation might somebody invite you to dance with the words *tixtieq tiżfen miegħi*?

8. *Buscarle tres patas al gato* is a Spanish idiom meaning splitting hairs or complicating matters unnecessarily, but how does it translate literally?

9. What vegetables are called *die Kartoffeln* in German?

10. In which language were some of J K Rowling's novels published under the titles *Harry Potter ve Zümrüdüanka Yoldaşlığı*, *Harry Potter ve Ölüm Yadigârları* and *Harry Potter ve Ateş Kadehi*?

11. What does the word *casa* mean in Italian, Spanish and Portuguese?

12. In what country would you be likely to hear the expression *päästää sammakko suusta* in reference to someone who puts their foot in it by saying the wrong thing? Literally translated, it means 'letting a frog out of your mouth'.

25 THE CALL OF THE WILD
Answers on page 200

1. The Kruger, Naroo and Addo national parks are in which country?

2. Which US national park beginning with Y is located in California?

3. Giant tortoises famously live on the Galápagos Islands, but there are in fact two living species of giant tortoise. Where can you find the other, with a population six times greater than their Galápagos cousins?

4. Komodo National Park was set up in the Lesser Sunda Islands in 1980 to protect Komodo dragons. Which country is this part of?

5. Which species of penguin lives right on the equator?

6. Native to west Africa, what type of creature are drills and mandrills?

7. What is the UK's northernmost (and largest) national park?

8. Which country is a popular wildlife destination boasting 5% of global biodiversity (despite being smaller than Lake Michigan), which has five active volcanos, generates 99% of its power from renewable sources and has no army?

9. Just 29 countries are larger than the world's biggest terrestrial national park! Where is this vast protected area located?

10. Estimates suggest African elephants may have numbered 27 million as recently as 1800, but how many are left today? 4 million, 2 million, 800 thousand, 400 thousand, or 80 thousand?

11. More than 100 species of lemur can be found only in the forests of which country?

12. Torres del Paine, Lauca and Laguna San Rafael are among the 41 national parks of which country?

13. How many humps does the Bactrian camel of central Asia have?

14. In which one of these countries do gorillas *not* live? Cameroon, DR Congo, Gabon, Rwanda, Uganda, Zambia.

15. On which island would you find Gunung Palung, Baku and Kinabalu national parks?

16. Which national park is said to contain half of the world's geysers?

17. Which one of these birds can fly? Cassowary, emu, great white pelican, kiwi, macaroni penguin, rhea, snoring rail.

18. There are two living species of alligator. One is found throughout the southern USA; in which country would you find the other?

19. The Great Migration is an annual movement of wildebeest between the Masai Mara in Kenya and which national park to its south?

20. The Great Barrier Reef, the world's largest coral reef system, is on which side of Australia? Northeast, southeast, southwest or northwest?

21. The world's largest rodent, the capybara, is native to which continent?

22. Established in the 1920s, Wood Buffalo National Park is the largest national park in which country?

23. Where would you find Plitvice Lakes National Park, a spectacularly photogenic forested reserve most famed for its chain of 16 terraced lakes joined by waterfalls?

24. What is the only species of bear that lives in South America – being famously the inspiration for Paddington (who hails from 'darkest Peru')?

25. If you were on a wildlife trip to see yellow-eyed penguins, tuataras, moreporks and keas, which country would you be visiting?

26 YOU GET THE NEXT ROUND
Answers on page 201

Match each nation listed below with their popular local beer.

1. Austria	**8.** India	**15.** Morocco
2. Belgium	**9.** Ireland	**16.** New Zealand
3. Belize	**10.** Italy	**17.** Portugal
4. Bolivia	**11.** Jamaica	**18.** Singapore
5. Colombia	**12.** Kenya	**19.** Thailand
6. Denmark	**13.** Madagascar	**20.** Turkey
7. Iceland	**14.** Mexico	**21.** Venezuela

A	B	C

D	E	F

27 DR LIVINGSTONE, I PRESUME?
Answers on page 201

Match each of these famous sites across the African continent with the locations marked A–L on the map below.

1. Baobab Avenue

2. Cape Town

3. Dakar

4. Kruger National Park

5. Lake Chad

6. Lake Malawi

7. Marrakesh

8. Mount Kilimanjaro

9. Nairobi

10. Okavango Delta

11. Suez Canal

12. Valley of the Kings

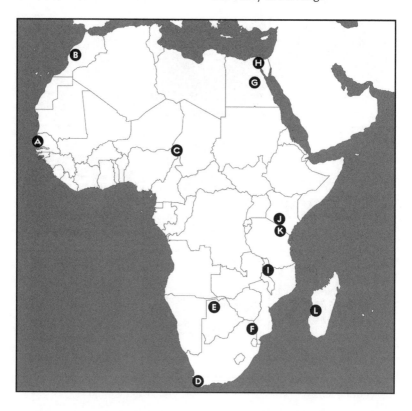

28 CHAIN REACTION
Answers on page 201

Each answer in this quiz is a country that borders the answers to the questions that immediately precede and follow it. Thus, the answers proceed in a geographical sequence of neighbouring nations.

1. The longest bridge in Europe is found here.

2. This kingdom produces more than a third of the world's olives, with a 6-million-tonne annual production of the crop that outweighs its human population more than two to one.

3. The motto of this country translates as 'liberty, equality, fraternity'.

4. Built between 1998 and 2008, the largest machine in the world straddles the international border between *answer 3* and this country.

5. The birthplace of actor and politician Arnold Schwarzenegger.

6. Inventor Ernő Rubik of Rubik's Cube fame comes from this nation.

7. The movies *War Dogs* (2016) and *The Nun* (2018) were shot here, as were large parts of controversial 2006 comedy *Borat*.

8. The name of this country's capital derives from the Greek for 'wisdom'.

9. There are provincial capital cities called Kars, Van and Batman here.

10. This country is the world's largest producer of saffron and pistachios, as well as a major producer of dates and honey.

11. Eight cities in this nation are more populous than its capital.

12. The international code for the currency used here is INR.

13. A nation that is divided into 14 states and regions, including Shan, Chin, Kachin, Kayin and Mandalay.

14. This mountainous landlocked country is one of the world's few remaining communist states.

15. The most famous of the three UNESCO World Heritage Sites in this country features prominently on its red-and-blue national flag.

29 WORDS OF WISDOM
Answers on page 201

Take a trip around the world through the immortal words of famous thinkers, activists, leaders and scientists.

1. The well-known 19th-century speech comprising just 271 words and opening with 'Four score and seven years ago...' was delivered in which city?

2. What was the nationality of the great man who said these words in a speech in Geneva? 'I regard myself as a soldier, though a soldier of peace.'

3. 'I think, therefore I am' – famous words from the writings of one who has often been called the Father of Modern Philosophy. What country was he from?

4. Which world-famous scientist said these words in a 2007 interview? 'The downside of my celebrity is that I cannot go anywhere in the world without being recognised. It is not enough for me to wear dark sunglasses and a wig.'

5. Complete the words of US President John F Kennedy that he addressed to a crowd of 120,000 in 1963: 'Two thousand years ago, the proudest boast was *civis romanus sum*. Today, in the world of freedom, the proudest boast is ___ ___ ___ ___.'

6. Which leader famously made the following rousing speech? 'We shall fight on the beaches; we shall fight on the landing grounds; we shall fight in the fields and in the streets; we shall fight in the hills; we shall never surrender.'

7. In a 2013 address to the UN, who said these inspiring words on her 16th birthday? 'Let us pick up our books and pens. They are our most powerful weapons. One child, one teacher, one book and one pen can change the world.'

8. The famous 'I Have a Dream' speech by African American minister and civil-rights activist Martin Luther King Jr was delivered in front of a 250,000-strong crowd in which city in 1963?

9. Which author made the following observation in a 1992 book? 'A common mistake that people make when trying to design something completely fool-proof is to underestimate the ingenuity of complete fools.'

10. Who spoke the words 'That's one small step for [a] man, one giant leap for mankind' before making the first-ever human footprint on the surface of the Moon?

11. These were reportedly the last words of which philosopher on his deathbed in London in 1883? 'Last words are for fools who haven't said enough!'

12. In what city was the author of these words writing in June 1942? 'Writing in a diary is a really strange experience for someone like me. Not only because I've never written anything before, but also because it seems to me that later on neither I nor anyone else will be interested in the musings of a 13-year-old schoolgirl.'

13. Who is credited with saying these words? 'When a man sits with a pretty girl for an hour, it seems like a minute. But let him sit on a hot stove for a minute and it's longer than any hour.'

14. Which famous figure gave a three-hour speech that concluded with the following words? 'It is an ideal which I hope to live for and to see realised. But, my Lord, if needs be, it is an ideal for which I am prepared to die.'

15. Who said the following to the UN General Assembly in 2019? 'People are suffering. People are dying. Entire ecosystems are collapsing. We are in the beginning of a mass extinction. And all you can talk about is money and fairy-tales of eternal economic growth. How dare you!'

30 GOING ROUND THE TWIST
Answers on page 201

Enter the answers to the numbered clues into the spiral grid, from the outside inwards. Each answer shares its final letter with the first letter of the next answer. The boxes for the first and last letters of each answer (where the answers overlap) are shaded grey.

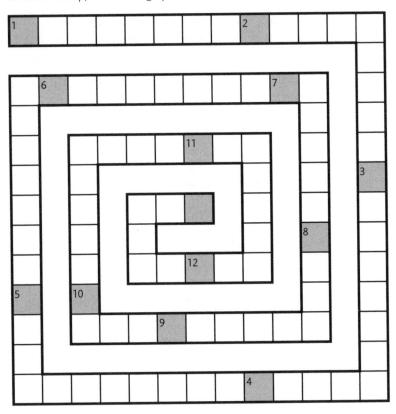

Once you have completed the spiral, rearrange the letters from the 13 shaded boxes to find the name of a sea that was an important trade route in ancient times and which is nowadays very popular with holidaymakers.

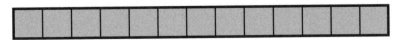

The number of letters in each answer is given in brackets after the clue.

1. Located in the north of England, this one-time major shipbuilding hub on the banks of the River Tyne is home to locals colloquially known as Geordies. (9)

2. The natural phenomenon that ultimately led to the disaster at Japan's Fukushima Daini nuclear power plant in 2011 (10)

3. One who studies mummified remains, the ancient pyramids, hieroglyphic scripts and associated cultures, for instance (12)

4. A region of Romania in the Carpathian Mountains, strongly associated in modern popular culture with Bram Stoker's Count Dracula and other vampires (12)

5. The country with the dubious distinction of having the highest number of fatal shark attacks in the world, according to official statistics (9)

6. The top native predator in the Florida Everglades (9)

7. In traditional Italian cuisine, small pasta envelopes containing a minced meat or vegetable filling, typically served in broth or with a sauce (7)

8. Designed by Greek architect Constantinos Apostolou Doxiadis, this city was built in the 1960s to replace Karachi as Pakistan's capital (9)

9. A city in eastern France famed for its mustard, in which the usual ingredient of vinegar is replaced with white wine or wine vinegar to give a sharper and fuller flavour that is less astringent than other mustards (5)

10. An 1892 Russian ballet with a score by Pyotr Ilyich Tchaikovsky, a 20-minute suite from which has since become one of the best-known pieces of classical music (10)

11. Europe's largest seaport, with a population of more than 650,000, and home to professional football clubs Feyenoord, Sparta and Excelsior (9)

12. This overseas department and region of France is an island in the Comoros archipelago, located in the western Indian Ocean (7)

31 A ROSE BY ANY OTHER NAME
Answers on page 201

1. Which island's lush vegetation earns it the sobriquet 'The Emerald Isle'?

2. For which city is 'The Big Easy' a ubiquitous alias?

3. 'Land of Fire and Ice' is a phrase that typically refers to which country?

4. What has been known as 'The Eternal City' for more than two millennia?

5. Which country is called 'The Bread Basket of Europe'?

6. Which large city is frequently abbreviated to 'Brum'?

7. 'The Rainbow Nation' was coined in 1994 in reference to which country?

8. Once famed for its jute, jam and journalism, which city's heritage has been known as 'The Three Js' for more than a century?

9. For which nation is 'The Land of Poets' a common alias?

10. 'The Windy City' has been used to refer to which city since at least 1876?

11. Which country markets itself with the moniker 'Land of a Thousand Lakes' (an understatement by a factor of more than a hundred)?

12. 'Vegas of the East' is an epithet applied to which autonomous region?

13. The mainland of which country is often called 'The Hexagon'?

14. Popularised in the 1920s, 'The Big Apple' is the nickname of which city?

15. Which island nation is known as 'The Land of the Long White Cloud' – a loose translation of its native name?

16. Which capital is known as 'The Fair City'?

17. Which country is referred to as 'The Red Island', for its laterite-rich soils?

18. Which city is sometimes called 'Lion City', a literal translation of its name?

19. 'The Great White North' is an alternative name for which nation?

20. 'Tassie' is a nickname used for which island?

32 BY POPULAR DEMAND
Answers on page 201

The countries below all have very different population sizes, ranging from
4.8 million to 271 million. Match each country with the bar on the chart that
represents the size of its population.

1. Canada

2. Egypt

3. Indonesia

4. Netherlands

5. New Zealand

6. Nigeria

7. Portugal

8. Russia

9. South Korea

10. United Kingdom

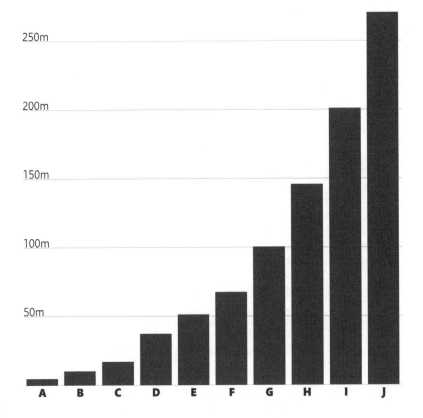

33 THIRTY-THREE
THREE-WORD ANSWERS
Answers on page 201

Each answer to the questions below comprises three words with the given initial letters. (In some cases the words may be joined with hyphens.)

1. What ANC is a huge Eastern Orthodox church in Sofia, Bulgaria?

2. What ASD is Japan's most popular beer?

3. What BOB is the body of water into which France's longest river flows?

4. What BOS is one of Venice's most popular tourist landmarks?

5. What CFF is an annual French celebration of movies?

6. What DES is the sixth most populated city in Africa?

7. What EFF is the world's largest celebration of the arts, held each August?

8. What ENP is a popular natural reserve in Namibia, home to lions, leopards, elephants, giraffes and zebras?

9. What GBR is a marine protected area encompassing the world's most extensive coral ecosystem?

10. What GGB connects San Francisco with Marin County?

11. What GGG is the scientific name of Gabon's most famous animal?

12. What HAC is the London Underground line connecting West Ham station with Euston station?

13. What HOW is a Welsh town famed for its bookshops?

14. What IOS is an archipelago that includes Tresco and St Martin's?

15. What JBI is a popular nickname for Khao Phing Kan in Thailand?

16. What JFL is an annual comedy festival held in Montreal?

17. What LAP is the famous orchestra that is based at Walt Disney Concert Hall in California?

18. What LVR is a popular Nevada-based NFL team?

19. What LWT is the tallest building in South Korea?

20. What PAP is a Caribbean capital city?

21. What PEI is a Canadian Maritime province?

22. What RAM is the national airline of Morocco?

23. What RBR is a Grand Prix race track located in Austria?

24. What RCI is the cruise line that operates ships including *Harmony of the Seas*, *Voyager of the Seas* and *Empress of the Seas*?

25. What RDJ is the home of the world's most famous carnival?

26. What SOH is an iconic building designed by Danish architect Jørn Utzon, and built between 1959 and 1973?

27. What SOL is a US landmark gifted by the people of France in 1886?

28. What TDC is the most remote inhabited archipelago in the world?

29. What TMR connects China to Russia via an ancient tea-caravan route?

30. What USF is an Orlando amusement park with a film and TV theme?

31. What VGM is a Dutch art gallery in Amsterdam?

32. What WAM is the name of an influential composer born in 1756 in Salzburg, Austria?

33. What WOW is a music festival held each August since 2007 in Gothenburg, Sweden?

34 DOUBLE DUTCH
Answers on page 202

Many languages besides English are written with the Latin alphabet, but that doesn't always make them easy for travellers to understand. Luckily, you don't need to translate the warning signs depicted below (unless you want bonus points!) but just to identify the language that each one is written in.

1

MATIÈRES
INFLAMMABLES!
DÉFENSE DE FUMER

2

BAWAL
MAGTAPON NG
BASURA

3

ATTENZIONE!

PERICOLO DI
CADUTA IN MARE:
TENERSI LONTANO

4

PRECAUCIÓN!

RESBALOSO
CUANDO ESTA
MOJADO

5

VAROKAA
HEIKKOJA JÄITÄ JA
LAIVAVÄYLIÄ

6

PASOP VIR
SEEKOEIE

7

UWAGA!
PŁAZY NA DRODZE

8

DİKKAT!
KÖPEK VAR

9

BETRETEN DER
RASENFLÄCHE
VERBOTEN!

10

THẬN TRỌNG!
KHÔNG ĐƯỢC ĐI
QUA

11

ATENÇÃO!
PROIBIDO
ESTACIONAR:
CARGA E
DESCARGA DIA E
NOITE

12

VARÚÐ!
SVÆÐIÐ ER
LOKAÐ ALLRI
UMFERÐ VEGNA
STÓRHÆTTULEGR
A HVERA

13

FIGYELEM!
KAMERÁVAL ÉS
KUTYÁVAL
ŐRZÖTT TERÜLET

14

ER LLES IECHYD Y
CYHOEDD
PEIDIWCH A
BWYDO'R
GWYLANOD

15

POZOR!
HRANIČNÍ PÁSMO:
VSTUP JEN NA
POVOLENÍ

16

PUTIM ON HEDLAIT
BILONG YU

35 THE SPANISH INQUISITION
Answers on page 202

1. The Alhambra is a palace and fortress complex located in which city?

2. Which Spanish painter and sculptor, born in 1881, is known for co-founding the Cubist movement?

3. What is the capital city of Catalonia?

4. Which of these is *not* one of Spain's autonomous communities (official administrative regions)? Andalusia, Castelo Branco, Catalonia, Murcia, Navarre.

5. Which of these Spanish cities is furthest north? Barcelona, Bilbao, Málaga, Seville, Valencia.

6. Majorca is the largest island of which Spanish archipelago?

7. Costa Brava is an area of northeast Spain that is popular with tourists, but what does the name mean?

8. Founded in 1927, what is Spain's flag carrier airline called?

9. Which of these islands is *not* Spanish? Formentera, Ibiza, Lanzarote, São Miguel, Tenerife, Trocadero.

10. Not counting the British Overseas Territory of Gibraltar (as it is not a country in its own right), with how many countries does mainland Spain share land borders?

11. What was the name of the Spanish currency used from 1868 to 2002?

12. Which mountain range is a popular skiing destination and home to Mulhacén, the highest mountain of continental Spain?

13. Europe's longest high-speed rail system (and the second-longest in the world after China's) connects Madrid to Barcelona, Alicante and Córdoba. What is it called?

14. Which of these is Spain *not* credited with first inventing? The ballpoint pen, Molotov cocktails, the mop, powered submarines, the wheelchair.

15. Mahon is the capital of which Spanish island?

36 PIGS MIGHT FLY
Answers on page 202

Of the ten thousand bird species with which we share our planet, most are masters of the art of soaring through the air, with many of them regularly undertaking quite epic airborne migrations. But there's a handful of birds that are no more capable of taking to the skies than the proverbial pig. Match each of these flightless species with their home on the map below.

1. Cape penguin

2. cassowary

3. dodo *(extinct)*

4. elephant bird *(extinct)*

5. emu

6. flightless cormorant

7. greater rhea

8. Humboldt penguin

9. invisible rail

10. kiwi

11. Lord Howe woodhen

12. ostrich

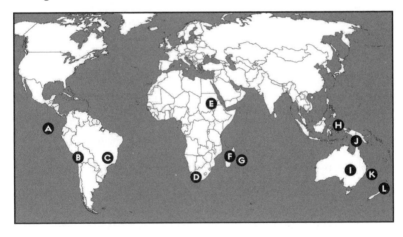

37 STAYING ON TRACK
Answers on page 202

1. By what English name are the Shinkansen high-speed trains of Japan colloquially known in English?

2. Which of these is not a railway terminus in central London? Kings Cross, Liverpool Street, New Street, Paddington, Victoria, Waterloo.

3. The busiest railway station in the world, in terms of the number of passenger movements, is Shinjuku station. In which city is it located?

4. Which long-distance passenger service, launched in 1883, connected Paris with Istanbul (then known as Constantinople)? Various alternative routes to cities such as Bucharest, Budapest, Vienna, Athens and Venice also existed over the years to 2009, when it ceased operating.

5. Which US train station holds the world record for the largest number of platforms, with a total of 44?

6. The world's third-longest rail line, the Trans-Siberian Railway has connected which city with Vladivostok since 1916?

7. In which country would you find Aluthgama railway station?

8. The Bilaspur-Leh line in India will be the world's highest when construction is completed but, until then, in which country can you find the only operational railway above 5,000m (16,400 ft)?

9. The TGV is the intercity high-speed rail service of which country?

10. What is the name of the railroad sleeper cars that operated on most US railroads for well over a century from their introduction in 1867?

11. Which of the following countries is the only one with an operational public railway network? Iceland, Iran, Libya, Malta, Yemen.

12. One of the world's most luxurious rail journeys, complete with butler service, the *Blue Train* is promoted as a 'moving five-star hotel'. In which country would you find this opulent 1,600km (994-mile) trip?

13. What is the name of the high-speed passenger-only service connecting the United Kingdom with France via a 50km (31-mile) sub-sea tunnel?

14. One of only three sleeper services in the United Kingdom, the *Night Riviera* operated by Great Western connects London with which town?

15. The main train station of which capital city is unofficially known as Hua Lamphong station?

16. In which country would you find the *Train to the Clouds*? The eight-hour journey includes 29 bridges, 21 tunnels, 13 viaducts, two spirals and two zigzags. It was built a century ago but is now run primarily for tourists.

17. In which city would you find the exuberant Italian-Gothic-style Chhatrapati Shivaji Maharaj Terminus, built between 1878 and 1887?

18. Between which two countries does a railway cross a 12km (8-mile) channel of water, spanning it partway by the Öresund Bridge and the rest of the way by the Drogden Tunnel? (The trains switch between bridge and tunnel on an artificial island created in the middle.)

19. The *Red Arrow* is an overnight sleeper train connecting the two largest cities of which country?

20. In which country would you find the Kuranda Scenic Railway, a short two-hour coastal journey cutting through Barron Gorge National Park?

21. Sirkeci railway station serves the largest city of which country?

22. What is the name of the holder of the world speed record for steam locomotives? It has held the title since 1938, when it achieved a speed of 203km/h (126 mph) during tests of a new type of brakes.

23. Prairie Dog Central Railway is a heritage line operating mainly on summer weekends in which country?

24. Which of these cities does not have trams/streetcars as part of its transport network? Berlin, Casablanca, Istanbul, Manchester, Prague, Singapore.

25. Voted the World's Leading Luxury Train every single year from 2012 to 2018 at the World Travel Awards, which service has capacity for 88 guests in 23 carriages, and runs on four routes covering more than 12 destinations across India?

38 GET YOUR MONEY'S WORTH
Answers on page 202

Across

8. Northeast African country (5)

9. South American river (7)

10. Currency trading system:
___ exchange (7)

11. Currency of India (5)

12. He who collected all the money in *8 across*, according to Genesis (6)

13. Peninsula where the Croatian kuna is used (6)

15. Give money in advance (6)

17. Country where lira is used (6)

20. Mother-of-pearl, used as early currency (5)

22. Currency used in Kabul (7)

24. Where a Scotsman might keep his money (7)

25. Dodge payment of taxes (5)

Down

1. Money gained dishonestly (4)

2. Island where the north is a de facto part of *17 across* and the south uses *21 down* (6)

3. Nation with capital Addis Ababa (8)

4. Currency used in *8 across* (5)

5. Currency used in *3 down* (4)

6. Metal used for coinage since 600BC (6)

7. Relating to money (8)

12. Nationality of those who use yen (8)

14. One who carries goods illicitly to avoid paying border taxes (8)

16. Pay via a third party (6)

18. Collectable silver Australian coins named for the arboreal marsupial depicted on them (6)

19. Deposits possessions as security for a loan (5)

21. Second most traded currency after US dollar (4)

23. Object, to buy or sell for instance (4)

39 CHALK AND CHEESE
Answers on page 202

Match these cheeses with their home nations:

1.	Coalho	Belgium
2.	Feta	Brazil
3.	Gorgonzola	Cyprus
4.	Gouda	France
5.	Gruyère	Greece
6.	Halloumi	Iran
7.	Lighvan	Italy
8.	Limburger	Mexico
9.	Manchego	Netherlands
10.	Monterey Jack	Poland
11.	Oaxaca	Spain
12.	Oscypek	Switzerland
13.	Roquefort	Turkey
14.	Tulum	United Kingdom
15.	Wensleydale	USA

40 WORLD LITERATURE
Answers on page 202

1. Children's author Roald Dahl was born in Cardiff, Wales, in 1916 to immigrant parents of what nationality?

2. First published in English in 1993, bestselling novel *The Alchemist* by Paulo Coelho was originally written in what language?

3. Who was the French author of *The Hunchback of Notre-Dame*, titled *Notre-Dame de Paris 1482* in the original version published in 1831?

4. In what language was *Crime and Punishment* originally written? It was first published in 1866 and translated into English two decades later.

5. What is the English title of the posthumously published novel by Stieg Larsson originally titled *Män Som Hatar Kvinnor* ('Men Who Hate Women') in Swedish? A movie adaptation was released in 2011.

6. What is the nationality of the author of the bestselling 2012 novel *The Travelling Cat Chronicles*?

7. Filled with allusions to literary works, music, films and paintings, *The Elegance of the Hedgehog* by philosophy teacher Muriel Barbery was first published in 2006 in which language?

8. *Don Quixote* – or *The Ingenious Gentleman Don Quixote of La Mancha* to give it its full title – is a classic Spanish novel sometimes considered to be the first modern novel. Who wrote it?

9. Pippi Longstocking is the main character in an eponymous series of children's books by Astrid Lindgren. What was Lindgren's nationality?

10. What is the English title of the novella, translated into more than 300 languages and dialects since its publication in 1943, by the French aristocrat Antoine Marie Jean-Baptiste Roger, Comte de Saint-Exupéry?

11. Who wrote the historical murder mystery *The Name of the Rose*, originally published in Italian as *Il Nome della Rosa* in 1980?

12. What was the original nationality of the author best known for his novels *The Unbearable Lightness of Being*, *The Book of Laughter and Forgetting* and *The Festival of Insignificance*?

41 LANDMARKS OF WESTERN EUROPE
Answers on page 203

Identify the famous sights depicted below and connect each one to its correct location on the map.

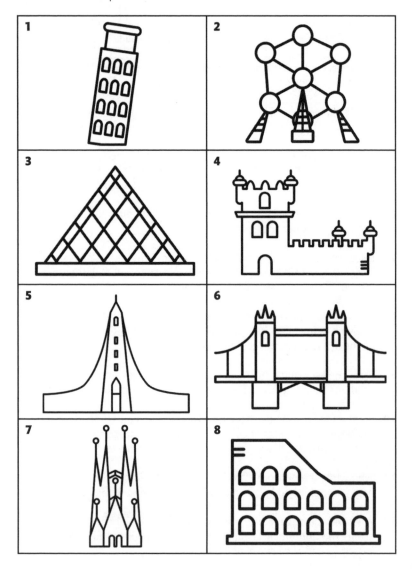

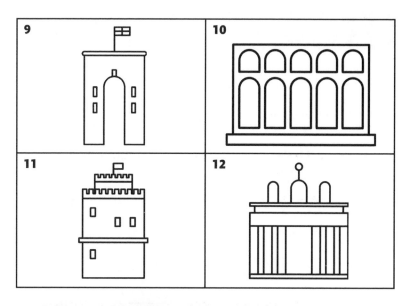

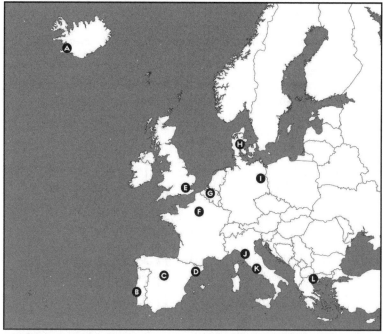

42 ALL SHOOK UP
Answers on page 203

Time for some anagrams. Rearrange the letters of the CAPITALISED word or phrase in each of the clues below to find the answer.

1. If you don't pay careful attention to the spelling, there is A DANGER of getting this Caribbean nation confused with a Spanish city.

2. People of this nationality live in the country that formed the largest part of the USSR IN A former era.

3. No doubt many have found ROMANCE on this Mediterranean island.

4. NOT A MAN should visit this state without seeing Glacier National Park.

5. The Vatican has many exquisite tourist sights, but this ornately painted hall is arguably the SHINIEST PLACE of all.

6. Among the highlights of this European capital are countless museums, beautiful canals, TRAMS, EDAM cheese, and nearly one million bicycles!

7. If it could speak, the demoniacally named marsupial native to this island might declare 'I AM SATAN'.

8. A good place to look for a brown BEAR IS IN the vast Russian province where the inhabitants are known by this term.

9. They presumably deem SALAMI BAD here, in the capital of a country where the sale and consumption of pork is mostly illegal.

10. Would you be scared to witness a violent STORM BOIL up while visiting this volcanic island, which has been erupting non-stop for centuries?

11. The summer climate of this capital city is very hot and oppressive, akin to the humid environment one finds in SAUNAS!

12. From one hot place to another: this is the old colonial name for a country where the HEAT IS HORRENDOUS in September and October.

13. These people SEEM NATIVE to a Southeast Asian country.

14. If you feel exhausted after a day walking around this Balkan capital city, you will be pleased to get back to the LARGE BED in your hotel room.

15. If you are looking for a restful CHANGE, OPEN your eyes to this destination, a picturesque capital city with a notably calm ambience.

16. Only the luckiest gambler SALVAGES his financial misfortunes here.

17. I DID RANT and rave when my trip to this beautiful Caribbean island was cancelled.

18. This scenic Canadian province offers a VACATION SO relaxing that you will almost certainly be left wanting to return there again.

19. I WANT A holiday in this Asian destination soon.

20. Animals you might see in this country include brown bear, wild boar, red deer, marmot, LIZARD, NEWTS, golden eagle and bearded vulture.

21. You could say this iconic American landmark was BUILT TO STAY FREE.

22. This is a classy place to stay in more than 500 locations around the world (HINT: HOTEL chain).

23. EEK! ALL GERMAN people have been under her leadership since 2005.

24. When the French colonised Madagascar, they seized the Malagasy queen's REGALIA and other belongings and banished her to this country, where she lived out her life in exile.

25. This capital city has something for everyone, whether you're a party ANIMAL, a foodie or an architecture buff.

26. It would be SAD, OVERALL, if you missed out on seeing this small nation in the Americas.

27. In the 1990s, extensive stabilisation works on this iconic Italian landmark offered much NEW HOPE FOR EASING A TILT.

28. Be careful not to LET MONKEYS IN your car when visiting Woburn Safari Park, located on the edge of this large Buckinghamshire town.

29. It's a disputed territory but there are no PENALTIES for visiting this place.

30. This composer has been called A FAMOUS GERMAN WALTZGOD – but technically he predates Germany and his birthplace is now in Austria!

43 A RIVER RUNS THROUGH IT
Answers on page 203

In the grid below, find the names of 21 famous rivers of the world. Words may run forwards or backwards in a vertical, horizontal or diagonal direction.

Y	A	N	G	T	Z	E	L	I	N
D	R	I	O	R	I	N	O	C	O
D	R	G	N	Z	E	N	I	E	S
A	A	E	A	D	A	N	U	B	E
W	Y	R	Y	N	U	M	O	T	R
A	G	L	O	V	G	S	A	H	E
R	C	O	N	G	O	E	I	A	R
R	H	U	D	S	O	N	S	M	I
I	Z	A	M	B	E	Z	I	E	O
E	U	P	H	R	A	T	E	S	L

44 BESIDE THE SEASIDE
Answers on page 203

1. In which country would you find the seafront suburb of Bondi Beach?

2. How many players are there in a beach volleyball team?

3. The famous Copacabana Beach stretches between two historic forts and is the usual official venue of the FIFA Beach Soccer World Cup. In which city is it located?

4. In which country would you find the black-sand beach of Perissa?

5. What spirit is the primary alcoholic ingredient in the cocktail known as Sex on the Beach?

6. What is the meaning of a half-red half-yellow flag on a beach?

7. Fossil-rich Lyme Regis sits on a 154km (96-mile) stretch of coastline in the south of England that is inscribed as a UNESCO World Heritage Site owing to its unique geology and geomorphology. What is it called?

8. Based on a 1996 novel by Alex Garland, *The Beach* is an adventure drama film directed by whom?

9. Waikiki Beach is located in which US state?

10. Which of these words does not mean 'beach' in a widely spoken language? Pelajar, plage, playa, praia, spiaggia, Strand.

11. In which country would you find Praia da Luz and Praia da Rocha?

12. Home to a colony of penguins since the 1980s, Boulders Beach is on the outskirts of which city?

13. Ha Long Bay is a UNESCO World Heritage Site and popular tourist destination in which country?

14. Which Tom Hanks movie was filmed on the beaches of Monuriki, one of the Mamanuca Islands in Fiji?

15. Flotsam and jetsam are both words describing debris from a ship, such as lost cargo, which may wash up on the shore. What is the key difference between the two?

45 LETTER TO THE EDITOR
Answers on page 203

At last week's publishing meeting, Commissioning Editor Claire gave the go-ahead for five new editions of Bradt guidebooks and each one has been assigned to a different editor. To use desk space in the editorial department more efficiently, the editors take it in turns to work from home one day per week.

Using the clues below, can you figure out the title and edition number of the book each editor is working on and which day they are out of the office? Complete the table using the logic grid to help you (by marking positive and negative relationships with ticks and crosses respectively). Each option in each category appears exactly once in the solution.

1. Laura is editing a book that has had 12 previous editions.

2. The guidebook for a South American country has been through one edition fewer than the other guide to a destination that's not an island.

3. The Guyana title has been assigned to a person (not Susannah) who isn't in the office on Mondays.

4. The person tasked with the Bradt Madagascar guidebook gets her turn to work from home right in the middle of the week.

5. As a big fan of spending all day in her pyjamas, Anna loves Thursdays, since that's when she can stay in bed and work from her laptop.

6. The Bradt Guide to the extraordinary island of Socotra is the editorial responsibility of Heather.

7. This edition of the guide to a semi-autonomous region of Tanzania will be the ninth.

8. The person managing the guide that contains a chapter on Muscat has to be at the office from Monday to Thursday.

			Guidebook					Edition					Home day				
		Guyana	Madagascar	Oman	Socotra	Zanzibar	1st	3rd	4th	9th	13th	Monday	Tuesday	Wednesday	Thursday	Friday
Name	Anna															
	Carys															
	Heather															
	Laura															
	Susannah															
Home day	Monday															
	Tuesday															
	Wednesday															
	Thursday															
	Friday															
Edition	1st															
	3rd															
	4th															
	9th															
	13th															

Name	Guidebook	Edition	Home day
Anna			
Carys			
Heather			
Laura			
Susannah			

46 NO MAN IS AN ISLAND
Answers on page 203

1. The island of Corsica is a region of which country?

2. What is the English name of the archipelago known in Spanish as Islas Malvinas?

3. What is the collective name of the archipelago that includes the islands of Mallorca, Menorca, Ibiza and Formentera?

4. Which is the largest island in the Caribbean?

5. Japan has almost 7,000 islands, more than 400 of which are inhabited. Tokyo sits on the largest and most populous of them. What is it called?

6. The islands of Comino and Gozo are part of which country?

7. Famed for its numerous moai – monumental statues in the form of giant heads – Easter Island is a Chilean territory in the Pacific Ocean. By what name is the island known to its inhabitants?

8. The cities of Catania and Palermo are found on which island?

9. Noël Coward, the British playwright and renowned wit who died in 1973, is buried on which island?

10. The towns of Waipahu, Kahului and Wahiawa are in which archipelago?

11. What is the name of the island in San Francisco Bay that housed a maximum-security prison from 1934 to 1963?

12. North Island, South Island and Stewart Island are the three largest islands of which nation?

13. On which island is the country of Brunei located?

14. Said to be the most remote inhabited islands in the world, which small British Overseas Territory is situated in the Atlantic Ocean, roughly midway between Africa and South America? The volcanic archipelago has no airstrip and the only means of access or escape for its population of 250 is by a six-day journey aboard a ship.

15. The islands of Lanzarote and Fuerteventura are part of which archipelago?

16. What was the nationality of the authors of *The Island of Doctor Moreau* (1896) and *Lord of the Flies* (1954)?

17. In which country would you find Rabbit Island, a small island populated with more than a thousand feral (but rather tame) rabbits, and also home to the sinister Poison Gas Museum since 1998?

18. Canada has three Maritime provinces: New Brunswick, Prince Edward Island and which other?

19. What is the name of the small tidal island located 1km (0.6 miles) offshore from northern France, where you will find an abbey and a small commune with dozens of historic buildings? The island, which features in the Bayeux Tapestry, is listed as a UNESCO World Heritage Site and receives more than 3 million visitors each year.

20. Which Indian Ocean archipelago merged with Tanganyika to form a single country, following a revolution in 1964?

21. Snake Island is a 43ha (106-acre) island that is home to thousands of highly venomous golden lancehead pit vipers, a species found nowhere else in the world. You might be happy to know that, for the protection of both reptiles and humans, it is not open to visitors other than scientists and the navy. In which country is this hair-raising place?

22. Which of these is not an island in New York City? Ellis Island, Galveston Island, Liberty Island, Manhattan Island, Roosevelt Island, Staten Island.

23. In which 1982 song – the music video for which was filmed in the Isles of Scilly – does Blondie sing 'Oh buccaneer, can ya help me put my truck in gear? Can ya take me far away from here? Save my soul from sin?'

24. New Providence Island, Great Abaco and Cat Island are all part of which country?

25. It was not until the 1840s that Hawaii came to be known to outsiders by its present name. Prior to that, it was known by what name, bestowed upon the archipelago by Captain Cook when he visited in 1778?

47 SAFETY IN NUMBERS
Answers on page 204

The answers to all of these general knowledge questions are numerical.

1. How many colours are on the Swedish flag?

2. In South America, how many sovereign states are there?

3. Through how many European countries does the prime meridian (Greenwich meridian) pass?

4. In China, how many time zones are there?

5. How many spikes are on the crown of the Statue of Liberty?

6. Chicago O'Hare International Airport has how many runways?

7. In French, what number is represented as 'quatre-vingt-seize'?

8. How many states (not counting territories) does Australia have?

9. With how many countries does Mexico share a land border?

10. Through how many countries does the River Douro flow?

11. How many living species of elephant are there in the world?

12. The names of how many US states begin with the letter O?

13. An overland journey from Pakistan to Greece via the minimum number of intervening countries would entail crossing how many international borders?

14. At the Palace of Westminster in London, how many hands does the clock of Big Ben have?

15. How many times has Argentina won the FIFA World Cup international football tournament?

48 EVERYBODY NEEDS GOOD NEIGHBOURS

Answers on page 204

Put the following countries in order of the number of neighbouring countries with which they share a land border – from zero to ten.

1. Brazil

2. Finland

3. Germany

4. Iraq

5. Madagascar

6. Peru

7. Portugal

8. Sudan

9. Tanzania

10. Thailand

11. USA

49 IN VINO VERITAS
Answers on page 204

France, Italy and Spain together produce more than half of the world's wine. Match the names on each of the bottles below with the wine-growing regions in and around these countries marked on the map.

1. Provence
2. Tuscany
3. Bordeaux
4. Rioja
5. Priorat, Catalunya
6. Sardegna
7. Mosel
8. Emilia-Romagna
9. Burgundy
10. Piedmont
11. Baden
12. Beaujolais
13. Tokaj
14. Minho
15. Champagne
16. Languedoc
17. Moravia
18. Puglia
19. Alentejo
20. La Mancha

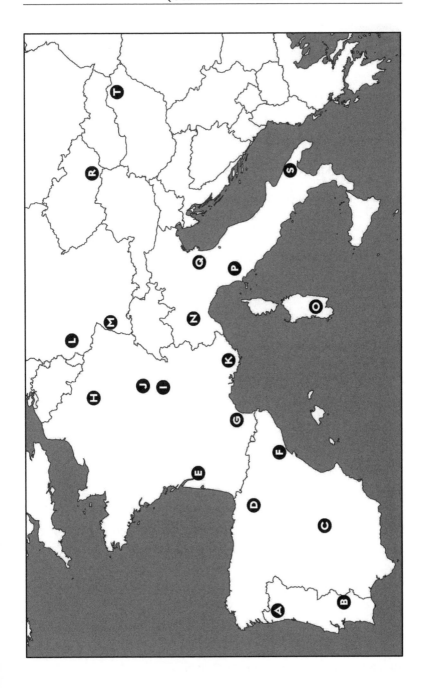

50 WONDERS OF THE WORLD
Answers on page 204

For each famous landmark listed, enter into the corresponding line of the grid the name of the city where it is located.

When completed, the shaded boxes will spell out vertically the name of one of the world's greatest attractions for sightseers.

1. Charles Bridge over the River Vltava

2. The Colosseum (Flavian Amphitheatre)

3. Brooklyn Bridge

4. El Rastro flea market

5. Van Gogh Museum on Museum Square

6. Musée d'Orsay Impressionist art gallery

7. Meiji Shrine (Meiji Jingū)

8. Hawa Mahal (The Palace of Winds)

9. Süleymaniye Mosque

10. Pushkin State Museum of Fine Arts

11. Doge's Palace

12. Palm Jumeirah artificial islands

13. Parc Güell

14. Millennium Stadium (Principality Stadium)

15. Forbidden City

16. Brandenburg Gate

17. Hagenauerhaus (Mozart's birthplace museum)

18. Kirstenbosch National Botanical Garden

51 HIDING IN PLAIN SIGHT
Answers on page 204

Many country names contain smaller words within them, such as 'law' in 'Malawi'. For each of the clues below, can you guess the word and then think of a country name that contains it? The number of letters in each hidden word is given in brackets.

Example: the answer to 'Man (4)' would be Argentina: the four-letter word meaning man is 'gent', and this is hidden inside 'Argentina'.

1. Sicilian volcano (4)

2. Not coastal (6)

3. Elegant water bird (4)

4. Wizarding tool (4)

5. Anaesthetic solvent (5)

6. Evergreen coniferous tree (4)

7. Lasting mark from a wound (4)

8. Forest clearings (6)

9. Numerous (4)

10. Underwater scuba forays (5)

11. Deep affection (4)

12. Sinister old women in folklore (6)

13. Outer coating of nutmeg (4)

14. Suffering or agony (4)

15. Southern African antelope (5)

16. Operatic solo (4)

17. Least dark (6)

18. Minute skin opening (4)

19. Frozen weather phenomenon (4)

20. Large yellow-fleshed root vegetable (5)

21. Pause expectantly (4)

22. Finished (4)

23. Craziness (5)

24. Enthusiasm (4)

25. Blemish (4)

52 MASAI MARA
Answers on page 204

Shade only the boxes containing letters that appear in 'Masai Mara' to reveal an evening scene from this magical African savannah region located in western Kenya.

M	A	M	Z	B	D	X	F	L	W	Q	C	D	U	O	V	T	U	D	X	L	V	D	B	L	L	Z	V	C	B
A	F	R	R	I	H	Z	P	Q	E	P	X	P	L	X	Z	G	X	G	O	O	G	E	E	S	X	N	W	H	H
R	M	M	R	M	R	S	T	U	F	U	W	E	E	E	X	K	Q	C	Y	P	P	S	E	J	M	I	O	H	J	N
I	S	A	M	A	I	I	I	I	I	S	U	J	Z	K	F	G	L	Y	B	T	G	E	S	I	R	R	F	V	B	E
I	R	R	S	U	I	A	S	M	R	R	I	S	R	U	Y	X	D	C	E	W	M	M	R	I	R	I	V	Z	N
Y	A	M	A	S	I	M	S	M	S	A	F	A	M	M	H	P	L	L	V	M	M	R	R	M	A	S	M	E	W
A	S	R	R	I	I	R	U	M	M	S	R	M	M	A	R	Z	Z	Z	F	I	A	A	R	F	R	A	M	R	R	N
D	A	A	I	I	S	A	M	R	I	I	R	M	A	R	I	M	I	O	A	I	S	U	P	W	X	Z	R	A	O
A	S	R	I	W	M	M	M	A	R	A	I	A	R	S	D	S	I	S	R	M	A	A	X	L	W	O	Z	Z	V	C
W	F	S	P	E	A	R	M	V	M	M	R	I	S	I	R	S	S	R	I	I	I	U	F	H	B	U	Z	U	E
B	S	S	C	M	A	I	A	I	I	A	M	I	M	M	A	R	M	R	R	A	J	L	B	X	X	J	P	Z	Q
R	S	X	I	S	A	B	F	G	N	F	A	Y	M	R	A	S	S	A	M	A	I	J	X	E	X	E	U	B	K
I	U	M	I	D	C	X	T	Q	W	F	Y	Z	L	B	A	R	S	A	M	R	A	S	E	Z	L	Z	L	O	G
I	M	A	E	K	Q	U	U	O	X	W	B	E	V	I	A	S	I	S	M	M	E	I	R	Q	B	Q	J	T	F
A	S	W	B	F	Q	O	P	W	F	O	C	H	A	I	I	R	R	S	R	P	S	M	R	M	L	C	F	J	B
M	D	U	G	Q	T	U	O	O	X	Y	N	A	I	R	I	R	M	A	S	L	K	D	M	G	X	E	G	V	Y
I	T	D	H	L	U	D	V	N	Z	A	A	R	I	I	R	I	R	I	B	Z	D	V	F	P	L	U	P	W	O
F	E	B	U	W	W	I	A	S	I	R	R	I	A	R	S	M	A	S	U	G	Y	E	Y	N	Z	N	U	D	E
V	D	E	B	A	S	I	R	A	I	I	M	R	R	I	A	I	A	R	T	H	H	N	V	U	E	O	D	W	P
F	G	L	S	S	A	R	I	M	I	R	I	M	R	I	A	I	R	S	R	P	I	E	M	Q	C	W	T	B	V
V	V	B	M	S	A	S	S	I	S	A	R	R	A	I	R	A	M	R	N	I	Q	M	C	I	Q	S	W	T	Z
V	C	C	A	M	S	I	R	M	S	S	A	A	R	R	R	R	A	R	R	Y	S	N	I	F	R	D	S	V	H
P	Q	U	R	A	I	I	I	M	A	S	I	S	A	A	A	A	S	I	D	S	T	A	C	I	G	S	C	A	H
N	N	I	M	M	A	S	I	M	R	M	S	U	B	M	R	S	I	K	I	J	M	B	S	Z	S	D	M	J	S
W	H	I	I	R	R	A	I	I	W	H	W	J	S	A	I	S	I	M	F	A	Q	M	W	I	Z	I	N	I	Q
Q	Q	I	Q	S	M	S	A	R	V	O	E	M	Q	M	A	R	R	W	S	G	A	B	M	U	I	D	M	T	A
E	X	R	U	S	R	S	S	Z	W	J	V	L	S	I	A	R	R	M	L	R	T	A	P	M	Z	S	B	M	X
C	S	A	E	R	M	I	I	B	Q	N	H	A	F	M	I	A	M	E	M	P	S	Z	M	B	I	G	I	Y	A
J	S	X	K	A	S	R	S	E	P	H	L	C	R	A	S	I	M	S	P	R	Q	S	Q	R	Y	I	H	M	D
N	R	G	T	A	A	A	S	K	J	C	P	I	N	R	S	R	I	S	R	V	S	D	A	K	M	D	I	P	R
G	V	P	W	A	I	Y	S	R	J	E	Z	H	A	I	M	J	I	S	X	I	C	R	J	A	Z	R	V	I	I
C	N	J	B	R	M	O	R	S	N	D	G	L	A	M	A	I	R	M	M	C	M	B	I	S	R	S	S	M	S
M	A	S	A	M	I	R	R	S	R	D	G	K	S	M	S	U	I	R	J	A	S	A	I	S	S	I	A	I	A
R	I	M	I	M	R	S	S	A	S	I	M	A	M	R	R	S	M	I	A	I	S	M	R	M	M	I	S	R	I
S	R	M	I	A	R	R	S	R	S	I	M	A	M	M	S	R	M	A	S	R	A	R	A	I	A	M	M	R	S
M	S	M	A	R	I	I	R	A	R	R	A	A	I	S	M	R	A	S	M	M	R	M	R	I	S	M	M	R	M
S	M	S	R	R	I	R	A	I	R	S	M	M	R	R	R	S	I	I	I	M	M	M	R	A	I	S	I	R	A

53 IN GOOD FAITH
Answers on page 204

1. Which French medieval Catholic cathedral suffered a devastating fire in April 2019, prompting a massive emergency response involving 400 firefighters and a subsequent pledge from president Emmanuel Macron that the damage will be repaired by 2024?

2. By what name is the Gothic Collegiate Church of St Peter at Westminster better known? It is the burial site of such famous figures as Rudyard Kipling, Geoffrey Chaucer, Charles Darwin, Samuel Johnson and Isaac Newton, as well as the interred ashes of Stephen Hawking.

3. In which city would you find the Hagia Sophia, built originally in AD537 as an Eastern Orthodox church then converted to a mosque in 1453, before being secularised in 1935 and established as a museum? In mid-2020, it was controversially reopened as a mosque.

4. Constructed in 1957, what is most notable about the design of the Roman Catholic Chapel of the Holy Cross in Sedona, Arizona?

5. Founded in AD597, and largely rebuilt in the Gothic style following a major fire in 1174, which is the mother church of the worldwide Anglican Communion?

6. Which world-famous mosque is centred on a building called the Kaaba (or Ka'bah)?

7. Featuring exotic opulent design and gold ground mosaics, St Mark's Basilica is one of the best-known examples of Byzantine architecture. Of which city did it become the official cathedral church in 1807 (a status which it retains to this day)?

8. By what name is Istanbul's Ottoman-era Sultan Ahmed Mosque more popularly known?

9. Construction began in 1882 on which large Roman Catholic church in Spain, which is currently scheduled to be completed in 2032 – after 150 years of work (with pauses for the Spanish Civil War and the coronavirus pandemic)? Its famous architect, who died in 1926, is buried in its crypt.

10. On a site equivalent to 200 football pitches in area, which temple complex in Cambodia is the largest religious monument in the world?

11. The Dome of the Rock is a shrine in a location of great significance not just to followers of Islam but also those of Judaism and Christianity. In which city would you find it?

12. The Transitional Cathedral in Christchurch, New Zealand, was rapidly constructed (using eight shipping containers for walls) after a 2011 earthquake destroyed much of the city's cathedral. By what name is it informally known, in reference to an unusual construction material?

13. Built between 1854 and 1859, and with a seating capacity of 3,000, the Dohány Street Synagogue is the largest synagogue in Europe. In the capital city of which country is it located?

14. What is the name of the Renaissance-style Papal Basilica in Vatican City, constructed between 1506 and 1626, and featuring a prominent dome designed by Michelangelo?

15. The Lotus Temple, so called because it is built in the form of a lotus flower, is a Bahá'í House of Worship in the capital city of what country? With an estimated 10,000 visitors a day, it is said to be one of the most-visited buildings in the world.

16. Built on the orders of Ivan the Terrible, St Basil's Cathedral – also known as the Cathedral of Vasily the Blessed and officially called the Cathedral of the Intercession of the Most Holy Theotokos on the Moat – is a distinctive architectural feature of which city?

17. Commissioned by Constantine the Great around AD327 in Bethlehem, and now a UNESCO World Heritage Site, what is the name of the church containing a grotto considered by several Christian denominations to be the birthplace of Jesus?

18. Comprising nine stacked platforms (six square and three circular) topped by a central dome, and decorated with 2,672 relief panels and 504 Buddha statues, Borobudur is the world's largest Buddhist temple. In which country would you find it?

19. What is the Kumano Kodō in Japan?

20. The Cathedral Basilica of the National Shrine of Our Lady Aparecida is the second-largest Catholic church in the world, by floor area. In which country would you find this impressive building?

54 FLYING THE FLAG
Answers on page 205

Match each of these national flags with the countries marked on the map opposite.

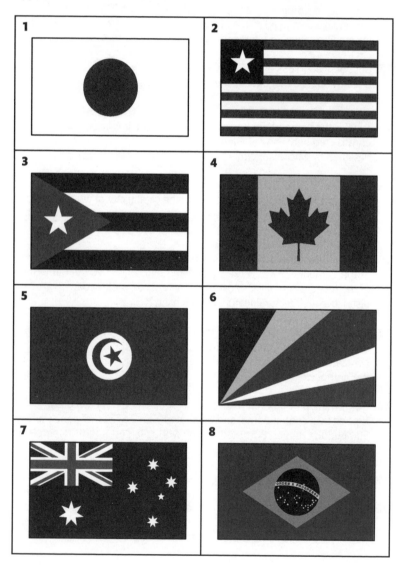

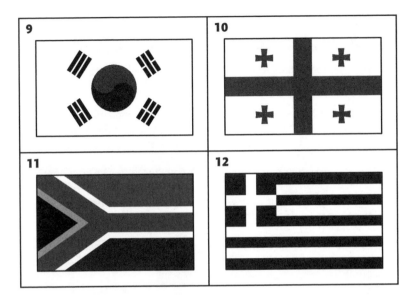

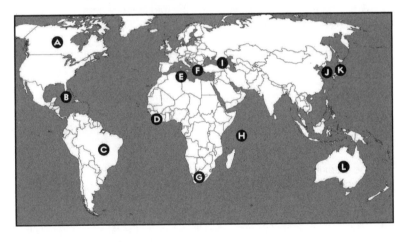

55 DRESSED TO KILL
Answers on page 205

1. The kimono is a traditional T-shaped garment, with square sleeves and a rectangular body, originating in which country?

2. What type of tasseled cylindrical hat, especially popular in the Ottoman empire, takes its name from the Moroccan city where the original dye used to colour the hats was extracted from red berries?

3. The poncho is an outer garment that originated on which continent?

4. Originating as peasant workwear, what is the name for the shorts with H-shaped braces now worn as traditional dress by men in Bavaria?

5. A long-sleeved tunic with ankle-length panels front and back, the áo dài is a national garment traditionally worn by the women of which country?

6. Where on the body would you wear the traditional Scottish item of clothing known as a tam o' shanter?

7. What is the name of the garment worn by women on the Indian subcontinent, which consists of a long cloth – typically around 6m (20 ft) in length – generally worn wrapped around the waist with one end draped over the shoulder, partially baring the midriff?

8. What is the English word for what are known locally as 'klompen' in the Netherlands?

9. The piupiu is a kind of skirt made of dried flax leaves and worn on ceremonial occasions by both men and women native to which country?

10. Which one of these Islamic headscarves covers the face, leaving only the eyes exposed? Al-amira, chador, hijab, khimar, niqab, shayla.

11. Derived from the Spanish word for 'shade', what is the name of the wide-brimmed sunhat that is particularly associated with Mexico?

12. What is the name of the traditional garment worn by indigenous women in Central America, comprising a loose-fitting tunic that is often heavily decorated with lace, ribbons and colourful embroidery?

56 ISLAND IN THE SUN
Answers on page 205

Match each of the islands listed below with the country that it is part of.

1. Baffin Island	Australia
2. Capri	Canada
3. Corfu	Cape Verde
4. Floreana Island (Charles Island)	Chile
5. Fraser Island	Denmark (Kingdom of)
6. Great Barrier Island	Ecuador
7. Hokkaido	Finland
8. Java	France
9. La Gomera	Greece
10. New Britain	Indonesia
11. Nosy Be	Iran
12. Qeshm Island	Italy
13. Réunion	Japan
14. Robinson Crusoe Island	Madagascar
15. Saaranpaskantamasaari	New Zealand
16. Sal	Norway
17. Socotra	Papua New Guinea
18. Spitsbergen	Spain
19. Streymoy	United Kingdom
20. Tresco	Yemen

57 TWIST OF FATE
Answers on page 205

Enter the answers to the numbered clues into the spiral grid, from the outside inwards. Each answer shares its final letter with the first letter of the next answer. The boxes for the first and last letters of each answer (where the answers overlap) are shaded grey.

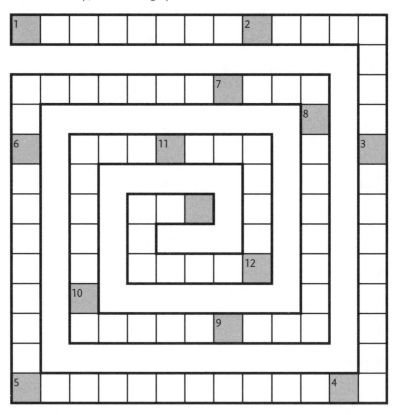

Once you have completed the spiral, rearrange the letters from the 13 shaded boxes to find the name of a small country headed by a prince.

The number of letters in each answer is given in brackets after the clue.

1. The US state, sometimes known as 'The Volunteer State', where you would find the cities of Knoxville, Clarksville and Nashville (9)

2. The hilly city, affectionately nicknamed 'Auld Reekie', that is home to institutions including the National Museum of Scotland, the National Library of Scotland and the Scottish National Gallery (9)

3. An Indo-Aryan language that is the lingua franca of northern India and Pakistan (10)

4. Prejudiced against Muslims (12)

5. A city in the USA, where Massachusetts Institute of Technology (MIT) is based, that was renamed in honour of a medieval university city in England in 1638 (9)

6. The embassy where WikiLeaks founder Julian Assange was holed up for seven years, claiming asylum, having absconded in breach of bail after his appeal against extradition was dismissed by the Supreme Court (10)

7. A mountainous country bordering the two most populous nations in the world (5)

8. An Italian luxury sports car brand that adopted a raging bull as its emblem and named many of its vehicles after Spanish fighting bulls (11)

9. Herbivorous lizards native to tropical areas of Central and South America, and the Caribbean (7)

10. The sedimentary rock type, typically composed of quartz or feldspar, from which Australia's Uluru (Ayers Rock) and South Africa's Table Mountain are formed (9)

11. A dish consisting of cooked edible land snails, often served as an hors d'oeuvre and typical of the cuisines of France, Germany and parts of Greece (8)

12. The nationality of people living in the city of Dodoma, around the Ngorongoro Crater area, or on the southern shores of Lake Victoria (9)

58 MENTAL MAP
Answers on page 205

Since the 1940s, experiments with rodents in mazes have demonstrated that they are extraordinarily adept at learning, remembering and manipulating mental representations of their spatial environment.

Let's see if you could hold your own against a rat's brainpower with these questions about world geography – no peeking at any maps or atlases till the end!

1. Which of the Great Lakes is nearest to New York City?

2. Through which three South American countries does the equator pass?

3. Switzerland shares a border with France, Italy, Germany and which two other countries?

4. If you sailed from Australia's west coast following the Tropic of Capricorn westwards, in which country would you be when you first encountered dry land?

5. Three friends – Lukas from Berlin, Gianna from Rome, and Martina from Madrid – decide to meet up for a weekend in Paris. Who has the longest journey, assuming they all travel by the most direct road route?

6. Which one of these countries has no coastline? Bolivia, Bosnia & Herzegovina, North Korea, Romania, Sudan.

7. A bird flies directly from the Turkish city of Istanbul to the Hungarian capital of Budapest; over how many other countries does it fly in between?

8. Which of these countries is more than double the size of the other four combined? Iran, Iraq, Jordan, Lebanon, Syria.

9. Driving from Ottawa to Panama City would be an epic road trip of some 7,600km (4,700 miles). What is the minimum number of intervening countries you would have to pass through along the way?

10. Which of these cities is furthest south? Brisbane, Buenos Aires, Cape Town, Durban, Santiago.

11. And which of them is furthest north?

12. What is the closest capital city to Vienna, as the crow flies?

13. Which is the largest of these Mediterranean islands? Corsica, Crete, Cyprus, Ibiza, Majorca, Malta, Sardinia, Sicily.

14. And which of them is the smallest?

15. Moldova is sandwiched between which two European countries?

16. Which country has the longest Red Sea coastline?

17. With which two countries does Nepal share a border?

18. Two aircraft take off simultaneously from Moscow and Tokyo, setting a direct course for the Indian capital of New Delhi. Assuming they both maintain the same ground speed, which one will arrive first?

19. Following the Mediterranean coastline of North Africa from west to east, put these countries in the order you would encounter them: Algeria, Egypt, Libya, Morocco, Tunisia.

20. In which country is the northernmost point of mainland Africa?

21. In which country is the southernmost point of mainland South America?

22. In which country is the easternmost point of mainland Asia?

23. In which country is the westernmost point of mainland Europe?

24. Sudan was the largest country in Africa until the 2011 secession of South Sudan. Now it sits in third place, behind which two countries?

25. Given that continental landmasses – which include Australia and Antarctica - are not classified as islands, what is the largest island in the world?

59 KNOW YOUR ONIONS
Answers on page 205

Match each of these French towns and cities with the locations marked A–I on the map below, and the same for the rivers J–L.

1. Bayeux

2. Chamonix

3. Le Havre

4. Lille

5. Lyon

6. Marseille

7. Nantes

8. Paris

9. Strasbourg

10. River Loire

11. River Rhône

12. River Seine

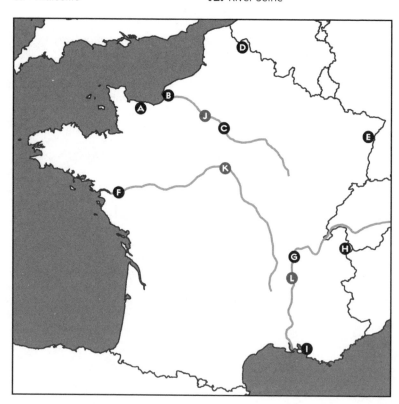

60 PIRATES OF THE CARIBBEAN
Answers on page 205

1. The three most populous Caribbean countries – with around 11 million people each – are Haiti, the Dominican Republic and which other?

2. What is the capital of Jamaica?

3. From which Caribbean nation does the street food 'doubles' originate?

4. What do Anguilla, Bermuda, the Caymans, Montserrat, the Turks and Caicos, and the Virgin Islands have in common?

5. Which country in the broader Caribbean region is an archipelago of more than 700 islands and has an economy that revolves around tourism and offshore investments?

6. Which Caribbean island nation is famous for 'The Pitons' – a pair of volcanic spires known as individually as Gros Piton and Petit Piton?

7. The so-called 'ABC islands' are three Dutch islands in the Leeward Antilles. The initials stand for Aruba, Bonaire and *what*?

8. Bridgetown is the capital of which Caribbean country, whose name literally means 'the bearded ones'?

9. Which comedic 1958 novel (subsequently adapted for film) set in Cuba was written by a former British Secret Intelligence Service agent and appeared to foretell the Cuban Missile Crisis of the 1960s?

10. Tourists flock to a world-famous beach on Big Major Cay in The Bahamas for the chance to swim with what animal?

11. What South American mainland country beginning with S is among those sometimes included as part of the Caribbean by virtue of their close political and cultural ties to the region?

12. Which Caribbean island was devastated in the 1990s by the eruption of its long-dormant volcano? As a consequence, the southern half of the island, including the capital, was designated an exclusion zone and to this day the whole population must live in the north.

61 GO WITH THE FLOW
Answers on page 205

1. Strasbourg, Cologne and Rotterdam are connected by which major river?

2. Which European river is the only one that has an officially designated long-distance walking trail running along its full length?

3. What is the longest river in Africa, and arguably in the whole world?

4. Which river was responsible for carving out the spectacular Grand Canyon in Arizona?

5. Austrian composer Johann Strauss II composed a waltz in 1866 about which European river?

6. Which river passes through the centre of the French capital city before descending northwest to meet the English Channel at Le Havre?

7. In which New York river was US Airways Flight 1549 famously ditched by Captain 'Sully' Sullenberger after bird strikes caused dual engine failure moments after take-off?

8. The longest river in Australia shares its name with an actor who stars in the 1993 comedy *Groundhog Day*, a British tennis player, and an energetic red-and-orange Muppet. What is it called?

9. What is the UK's longest river? There are other rivers with the same name in Australia, New Zealand, Canada and the USA.

10. Which river forms the natural border between the US states of Illinois and Missouri?

11. The Italian city of Turin is situated on the banks of which river? It shares its name with an animated panda, a female Teletubby, and the young protagonist of a 2016 movie directed by John Asher.

12. Which river flows over Victoria Falls in southern Africa?

13. Which Russian river, with a name literally meaning 'dampness' or 'moisture', flows 3,500km (2,200 miles) from the Moscow area to the Caspian Sea?

14. Asia's longest river is an anagram of GET ZANY. What is it called?

15. Found throughout the Middle East and North Africa, what is a 'wadi'? Examples include Wadi Bani Khalid in Oman, Wadi Rum in Jordan, and Wadi Al-Batin in Saudi Arabia and Kuwait.

16. Which of the world's rivers carries the largest volume of water? It discharges more than 200,000 cubic metres per second – enough to completely refill the Dead Sea every eight days!

17. The name of which long-lived herbivorous animal derives from the Greek for 'horse of the river'?

18. The Ghaghara, Yamuna and Kosi rivers are tributaries of which sacred but heavily polluted river?

19. Which Canadian and Alaskan river is pronounced the same as the abbreviated form of University of Connecticut?

20. In what country would you find the Khwae Yai River referenced in the title of the 1957 war film *The Bridge on the River Kwai*?

21. The two major tributaries of the Nile have names that include colours. What are they called?

22. Which major South African river shares its name with a county and city in California, the nickname of the Netherlands national football team, and a multinational telecommunications company based in France?

23. The Tigris flows for most of its length through which country, where the river is known locally as the Dijlah?

24. Which is the only country in the following list where you would find a permanent river? Kuwait, Malta, Monaco, Saudi Arabia, Tunisia.

25. Which river rises at Mount Fumaiolo and flows southwards, past Rome, to meet the Tyrrhenian Sea at Ostia?

62 A NOVEL SETTING
Answers on page 206

Match each of the countries marked on the map with the popular book for which it provides the backdrop.

1. *The Bear and the Nightingale* Katherine Arden 2017	**2.** *The Blind Assassin* Margaret Atwood 2000 
3. *A Man Called Ove* Fredrik Backman 2012	**4.** *My Sister, the Serial Killer* Oyinkan Braithwaite 2018 
5. *The Good Earth* Pearl S Buck 1931	**6.** *Like Water for Chocolate* Laura Esquivel 1989 
7. *Girl, Woman, Other* Bernardine Evaristo 2019	**8.** *The Old Man and the Sea* Ernest Hemingway 1952 
9. *The Kite Runner* Khaled Hosseini 2003 	**10.** *One Hundred Years of Solitude* Gabriel García Márquez 1967 

11. *The No. 1 Ladies' Detective Agency* Alexander McCall Smith 1998	**12.** *The Thorn Birds* Colleen McCullough 1977 
13. *State of Wonder* Ann Patchett 2011	**14.** *The God of Small Things* Arundhati Roy 1997
15. *Between Shades of Gray* Ruta Sepetys 2011	**16.** *The Shadow of the Wind* Carlos Ruiz Zafón 2001

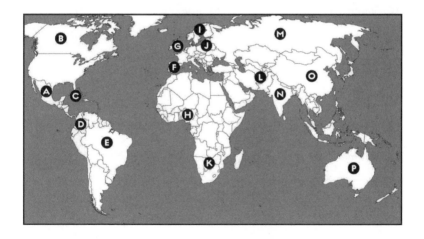

63 ALL FUN AND GAMES
Answers on page 206

Match these Olympic Games with their host cities:

1.	Summer 2016	Athens
2.	Winter 2014	Atlanta
3.	Summer 2012	Beijing
4.	Winter 2010	Berlin
5.	Summer 2008	Innsbruck
6.	Winter 2006	London
7.	Summer 2004	Paris
8.	Winter 2002	Rio de Janeiro
9.	Summer 2000	Salt Lake City
10.	Summer 1996	Sarajevo
11.	Summer 1988	Sochi
12.	Winter 1984	Seoul
13.	Winter 1964	Sydney
14.	Summer 1936	Turin
15.	Summer 1900	Vancouver

64 CAPITAL GAINS
Answers on page 206

From ASAP and FAQ to NASA and WWF, the world is awash with acronyms and initialisms. Test your knowledge of some international ones in this quiz.

1. What global organisation is abbreviated as IMF?

2. What does the P in OPEC stand for?

3. UNESCO is the United Nations organisation for the protection of world heritage, but what do the letters ESC stand for?

4. It is such a widely used term in the world of diving that SCUBA is nowadays generally accepted as a word in its own right, written lowercase, but what does the acronym stand for?

5. What does the A in NATO stand for?

6. Popular as internet slang since 2012, what does YOLO stand for?

7. UNICEF usually refers to itself as the United Nations Children's Fund, skipping the I and E, but what did those two letters originally stand for?

8. In what country would you find the political party ZANU–PF?

9. Every one of us owns a mobile phone with a SIM card nowadays, but do you know what SIM is short for?

10. How is the Russian acronym CCCP written in English?

11. By what acronym is the French state-owned railway system known?

12. The ANC is the governing party in South Africa. What does ANC mean?

13. Which capital city is colloquially referred to as KL?

14. In which of these common acronyms does the I not stand for 'International'? ICBM, IOC, ISBN, ISS, IUCN.

15. North Macedonia was initially admitted to the United Nations under the provisional name of FYR Macedonia. For what do these three initials stand?

65 WORLD KNOWLEDGE
Answers on page 206

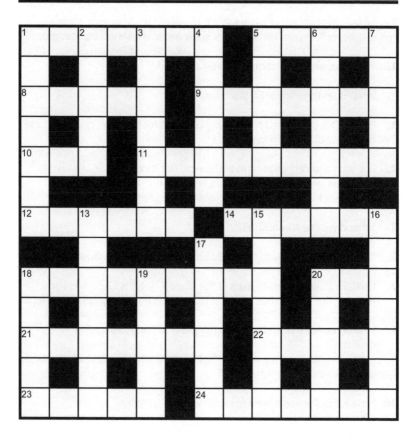

Across

1. Manuscript copyists of, for instance, *2 down* (7)

5. Carved pole typically representing family lineage (5)

8. Feat of engineering completed in 1914 in Panama (5)

9. City such as Tallinn, Tbilisi, Tehran, Tokyo or *24 across* (7)

10. Classic means of transfer from airport to city centre (3)

11. South American country led by Hugo Chávez from 1999 to 2013 (9)

12. Dairy product with name derived from Turkish; US spelling (6)

14. Ukrainian seaport on the Black Sea (6)

18. Indian Ocean island, home to Pamplemousses Botanical Garden and the Seven Coloured Earths (9)

20. French road (3)

21. The part of a church around the altar, typically occupied by the choir and priests (7)

22. Second most populous nation in the world (5)

23. Australia vs England cricket series typically held every two years (5)

24. City where Jomo Kenyatta International Airport is located (7)

Down

1. Part of a cruise ship one hopes never to visit (7)

2. Letters of Viking alphabet (5)

3. Currency of *11 across* (7)

4. Person following the leader in rock-climbing (6)

5. Very hard yellow to brown gemstone found mainly in Brazil, Russia and Nigeria (5)

6. Secures with a rope (7)

7. Valletta is capital of this island country (5)

13. Hungarian stew flavoured with paprika (7)

15. Colourful West African garment worn on upper body (7)

16. Native American tribe from northeast US and Quebec region (7)

17. Musical instrument for which Italian craftsman Antonio Stradivari is famed (6)

18. Destination of the Hajj annual Islamic pilgrimage in Saudi Arabia (5)

19. Early empire builders of Peru (5)

20. Cowboy riding contest (5)

66 KNOCKED FOR SIX
Answers on page 206

The answers to all of these general knowledge questions have six letters.

1. Which capital city, known in the local language as Baile Átha Cliath, is situated on a bay at the mouth of the River Liffey?

2. What is the name of the currency used in Israel?

3. Which country calls itself Druk Yul (literally 'Land of the Thunder Dragon'), its citizens Drukpa (the 'Dragon people') and the title for its head of state Druk Gyalpo (the 'Dragon King')?

4. The central Italian dish called zuppa inglese ('English soup') is a variation on which British dessert?

5. Which nation borders Luxembourg but not the Netherlands?

6. Which country uses national web domains ending in .ru and also, for historical reasons, .su?

7. Glacier Bay, Denali and Kenai Fjords are the most-visited of the national parks in which US state?

8. The Dead Sea straddles the border of Israel and which other country?

9. In which city would you find the football stadiums Santiago Bernabéu, Wanda Metropolitano and (until its closure in 2017) Vicente Calderón?

10. Which is the smallest of these countries, both by area and by population? Angola, Guinea, Malawi, Rwanda, Uganda, Zambia.

11. On which island would you find the cities of Larnaca and Limassol?

12. From which river does the Dutch capital city derive its name?

13. Also known as Kami-no-michi, what is the primary religion of Japan?

14. Which country on the Persian Gulf shares land borders with both Iraq and Saudi Arabia?

15. The Pindus mountain range is found in the northwest of which country?

67 THE AMERICAN DREAM
Answers on page 206

Match each of these renowned US places with the locations marked A–P on the map below, and the same for the rivers Q–T.

1. Beverly Hills

2. Brooklyn Bridge

3. Chicago

4. Disney World

5. Graceland

6. Grand Canyon

7. Hoover Dam

8. Houston

9. Kansas City

10. Miami Beach

11. Mount Rushmore

12. Niagara Falls

13. Sacramento

14. Seattle

15. The Pentagon

16. Yellowstone National Park

17. Colorado River

18. Hudson River

19. Mississippi River

20. Rio Grande

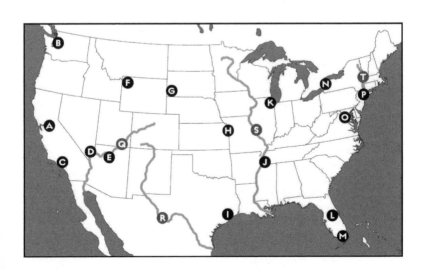

68 FACTS AND FIGURES
Answers on page 206

Below are ten sets of recent statistics about ten different countries. Can you match each country with its corresponding data profile?

1.	Brazil	**6.**	Sweden
2.	France	**7.**	Turkey
3.	Greece	**8.**	Ukraine
4.	Iran	**9.**	United Kingdom
5.	Singapore	**10.**	USA

A. · **Life expectancy:** 80.3 years
· **Smoking prevalence:** 22% of adults
· **Military expenditure:** 3.4% of GDP
· **Non-fossil energy sources:** nuclear 20%; wind & solar 3%; hydro 6%
· **Main religions:** Protestant 43%; Catholic 20%; no religion 27%

B. · **Life expectancy:** 72.9 years
· **Smoking prevalence:** 29% of adults
· **Military expenditure:** 3.9% of GDP
· **Non-fossil energy sources:** nuclear 54%; wind & solar 4%; hydro 3%
· **Main religions:** Orthodox 67%; Catholic 10%; no religion 11%

C. · **Life expectancy:** 86.0 years
· **Smoking prevalence:** 16% of adults
· **Military expenditure:** 3.2% of GDP
· **Non-fossil energy sources:** nuclear 0%; wind & solar 2%; hydro 0%
· **Main religions:** Buddhist 34%; Christian 18%; Muslim 14%; none 19%

D. · **Life expectancy:** 82.2 years
· **Smoking prevalence:** 33% of adults
· **Military expenditure:** 1.8% of GDP
· **Non-fossil energy sources:** nuclear 72%; wind & solar 4%; hydro 9%
· **Main religions:** Catholic 41%; Muslim 5%; Protestant 2%; none 40%

E. · **Life expectancy:** 75.7 years
   · **Smoking prevalence:** 27% of adults
   · **Military expenditure:** 1.9% of GDP
   · **Non-fossil energy sources:** nuclear 0%; wind & solar 10%; hydro 23%
   · **Main religions:** Muslim 78% (officially 99%); no religion 21%

F. · **Life expectancy:** 82.4 years
   · **Smoking prevalence:** 19% of adults
   · **Military expenditure:** 1.1% of GDP
   · **Non-fossil energy sources:** nuclear 40%; wind & solar 2%; hydro 53%
   · **Main religions:** Protestant 30%; Muslim 1%; no religion 67%

G. · **Life expectancy:** 74.7 years
   · **Smoking prevalence:** 14% of adults
   · **Military expenditure:** 1.5% of GDP
   · **Non-fossil energy sources:** nuclear 3%; wind & solar 2%; hydro 62%
   · **Main religions:** Catholic 60%; Protestant 27%; no religion 9%

H. · **Life expectancy:** 81.1 years
   · **Smoking prevalence:** 43% of adults
   · **Military expenditure:** 2.3% of GDP
   · **Non-fossil energy sources:** nuclear 0%; wind & solar 15%; hydro 12%
   · **Main religions:** Orthodox 89%; Muslim 2%; no religion 5%

I. · **Life expectancy:** 81.1 years
   · **Smoking prevalence:** 15% of adults
   · **Military expenditure:** 2.1% of GDP
   · **Non-fossil energy sources:** nuclear 18%; wind & solar 21%; hydro 2%
   · **Main religions:** Christian 39%; Muslim 5%; no religion 52%

J. · **Life expectancy:** 74.5 years
   · **Smoking prevalence:** 11% of adults
   · **Military expenditure:** 3.8% of GDP
   · **Non-fossil energy sources:** nuclear 2%; wind & solar 0%; hydro 5%
   · **Main religions:** Muslim 80% (officially 99%); no religion 19%

69 TOUR...NADO!
Answers on page 206

To be quite honest, things had already started to get into a muddle with this group tour from the word go, as all five participants had confusingly similar names. Barely ten minutes after everybody had introduced themselves to one another on arrival at the airport, the sparks truly began to fly when it transpired that they had all been charged grossly different prices for their flights. Tempers frayed further as each traveller realised that they had forgotten to bring something important and – to make matters still worse – it proved impossible to keep the whole group happy as they had all arrived with completely different expectations of the trip!

Using the clues below, can you figure out each person's particular special interest along with the item they left behind and how much they paid for flights? Complete the table using the logic grid to help you (by marking positive and negative relationships with ticks and crosses respectively). Each option in each category appears exactly once in the solution.

1. Jill, who had booked the trip in the mistaken belief that it was a yoga and meditation retreat, paid £100 less for her flights than the person who had absent-mindedly left their camera behind.

2. The traveller who came in full expectation of two weeks' birdwatching was charged the average price for flights.

3. The others refused to speak to Jed after discovering that he had, for no discernible reason, been given by far the best deal on his flights.

4. Jon spent much of the time sneering at the birder and mocking them for what he viewed as their 'tedious hobby'.

5. When the day set aside for visiting ancient monuments came, the person who paid £200 for flights spent the whole day sulking in their hotel room following a frankly embarrassing outburst over breakfast in which they declared monuments 'duller than drying paint'. Perhaps this was just as well, given that they had forgotten to bring a toothbrush and as a result were becoming increasingly unpleasant to be around.

6. On the tour bus, everyone kept at least two rows away from Jim who was developing an equally intriguing aroma, having neglected to pack any spare underwear in his suitcase.

7. Jen, who was pleased to learn she had not paid the steepest price for flights, was looking forward to seeing either volcanoes or monuments.

8. The person who had come along in vain search of parties and nightlife instead went home with a terribly sunburnt head owing to the fact that their hat had spent the entire two weeks sitting on their kitchen table.

		Special interest					Flight price					Forgotten item				
		Birding	Meditation	Monuments	Nightlife	Volcanoes	£100	£200	£300	£400	£500	Camera	Credit card	Sunhat	Toothbrush	Underwear
Traveller	Jed															
	Jen															
	Jill															
	Jim															
	Jon															
Forgotten item	Camera															
	Credit card															
	Sunhat															
	Toothbrush															
	Underwear															
Flight price	£100															
	£200															
	£300															
	£400															
	£500															

Traveller	Special interest	Flight price	Forgotten item
Jed			
Jen			
Jill			
Jim			
Jon			

70 FACE THE MUSIC
Answers on page 206

1. Which city completes the title of a song from the musical *Chess*, which debuted in the West End in 1986: *One Night in ___*?

2. The name of which African country is also the title of a song by the Red Hot Chili Peppers, featured on their 2011 album *I'm With You*?

3. Which nationality completes the title of the pop rock hit from the 1986 album *Different Light* by The Bangles: *Walk Like a(n) ___*?

4. Which city completes the title of a song by The Beautiful South from their album *Blue Is the Colour*, released in 1996: *___ (or Anywhere)*?

5. First recorded in 1969 by Ralph McTell (who updated it in 2020 with an extra verse inspired by the coronavirus pandemic), this song title is completed with the name of which city: *Streets of ___*?

6. The name of which country completes the title of Alphaville's 1984 hit from their *Forever Young* album: *Big in ___*?

7. Which city completes the title of a soulful 1968 pop song written and composed for singer Dionne Warwick by Burt Bacharach, with lyrics by Hal David: *Do You Know the Way to ___*?

8. The name of which island completes the title of the 1999 song by Dutch Eurodance group the Vengaboys: *We're Going to ___*?

9. Which city completes the title of a song written in 1953 and best known for the version released in 1962 by Tony Bennett: *I Left My Heart in ___*?

10. Which nationality completes the title of The Beatles song released on their album *Rubber Soul* in 1965: *___ Wood (This Bird Has Flown)*?

11. The name of which city completes the title of Michael Jackson's 1996 release, which he originally wrote as a poem while staying in that city on his Dangerous World Tour three years previously: *Stranger in ___*?

12. Which capital city completes the title of the Morrissey track, which he co-wrote with guitarist Boz Boorer, released on his album *Years of Refusal* in 2009: *I'm Throwing My Arms Around ___*?

71 ENDEMIC CREATURES
Answers on page 206

Match these animals with the place where they live:

1. Aldabra giant tortoise   Borneo

2. Amami rabbit   Pakistan

3. Asiatic lion   New Zealand

4. aye-aye   Indonesia

5. gelada   Lord Howe Islands

6. giant panda   Seychelles

7. golden lion tamarin   China

8. Indus river dolphin   Brazil

9. kakapo   Japan

10. Komodo dragon   Galápagos

11. marine iguana   Ethiopia

12. proboscis monkey   Madagascar

13. tree lobster   Australia

14. vaquita   India

15. wombat   Mexico

72 ON THE DOT
Answers on page 207

This is *Connect the Dots* reinvented for travel brainboxes! Several cities, towns and other places have been marked on the map of Central Europe. Each clue below identifies one of those locations. Connect each corresponding dot in sequence with straight lines to reveal a majestic creature. Not all dots are included in the solution.

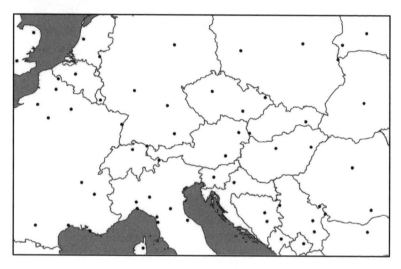

1. The Hungarian capital

2. The tripoint of Bulgaria, Romania and Serbia

3. Lozica Monastery in eastern Serbia

4. The city of Niš, 55km (34 miles) south of *point 3*

5. Gorna Oryahovitsa Airport, northern Bulgaria

6. Romania's capital city

7. Târgu Mureș in the heart of Transylvania

8. Ternopil, Ukraine

9. The tripoint of Belarus, Poland and Ukraine

10. The Polish capital

11. Leszno, a Polish town 137km (85 miles) from the German border

12. Magdeburg, a German city on the same latitude as Warsaw

13. De Maasduinen National Park on the Netherlands-Germany border

14. Lille

15. Bapaume, 60km (37 miles) south of point 14

16. The French village of La Feuillie, northwest of Paris

17. The Eiffel Tower

18. Reims, located between Luxembourg and the French capital

19. *Point 17 again*

20. The seat of the European Parliament

21. Lake Constance, at the tripoint of Austria, Germany and Switzerland

22. The tripoint of Austria, Italy and Switzerland

23. Bologna, capital of Italy's Emilia-Romagna region

24. *Point 22 again*

25. Piacenza Cathedral, northeast of Genoa and northwest of Bologna

26. Novi Ligure, north of Genoa

27. Italian port city of Genoa

28. *Point 23 again*

29. Vento Caves, 34km (21 miles) north of *point 30*

30. The Leaning Tower of Pisa

31. The enclave of San Marino

32. Graz, Austria

33. *Point 1 again*

34. Serbian border town of Badovinci

35. Ponijeri ski centre, north of Sarajevo

36. Capital of Bosnia and Herzegovina

37. *Point 4 again*

38. Danube's Big Boilers, on the Romania-Serbia border

73 MIND YOUR LANGUAGE
Answers on page 207

For each country listed, enter into the corresponding line of the grid the name of the most widely spoken language in that country.

When completed, the shaded boxes will spell out vertically a great piece of advice for travellers.

1. Malta

2. Cuba

3. Cameroon

4. Austria

5. Burundi

6. Andorra

7. Israel

8. Myanmar

9. San Marino

10. Papua New Guinea

11. Jordan

12. China

13. Ghana

14. Madagascar

15. Pakistan

16. India

17. Brazil

18. Laos

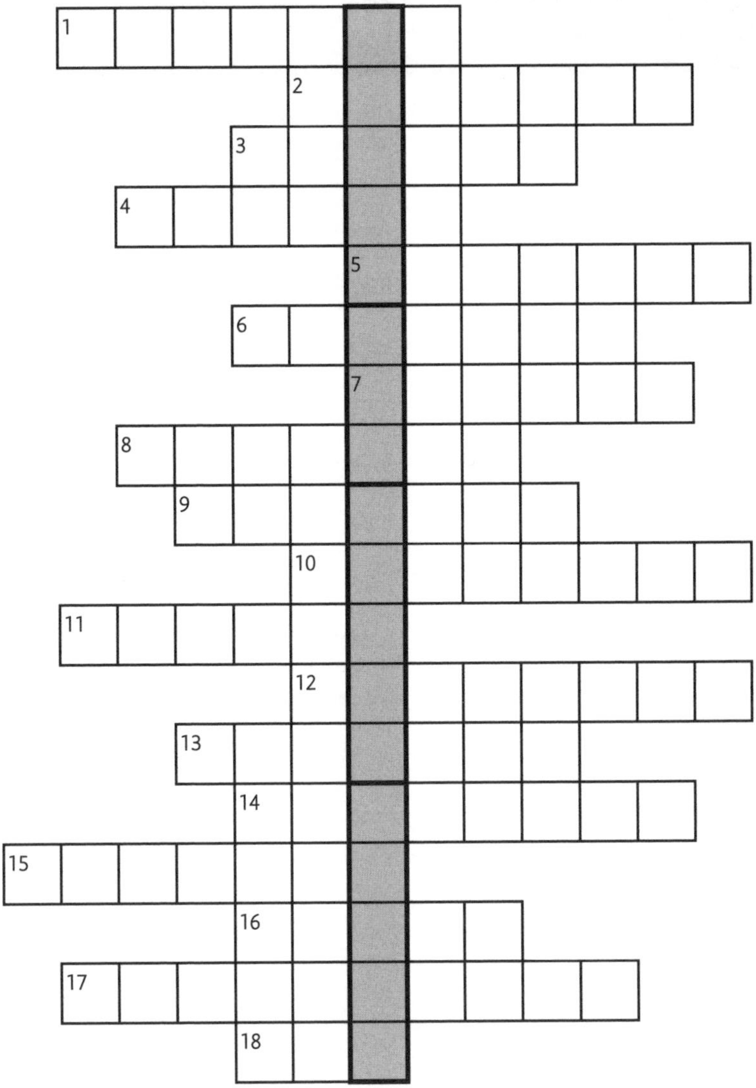
1
2
3
4
5
6
7
8
9
10
11
12
13
14
15
16
17
18

74 INDUSTRIAL STRENGTH
Answers on page 207

When it comes to international trade, different countries have different specialities. Match each of the commodities listed below with the country that is the world's largest producer.

1.	bananas	Australia
2.	cars	Brazil
3.	cashew nuts	China
4.	cherries	India
5.	cocoa	Indonesia
6.	coffee	Iran
7.	daffodils	Ivory Coast
8.	digital cameras	Japan
9.	military weaponry	Madagascar
10.	oats	Netherlands
11.	olives	Russia
12.	palm oil	Spain
13.	rubber	Thailand
14.	saffron	Turkey
15.	sunflower seeds	Ukraine
16.	tulips	United Kingdom
17.	vanilla	USA
18.	wool	Vietnam

75 A LOT IN COMMON
Answers on page 207

In this quiz, the object is to find pairs of countries that share not only a land border but also the initial letter of their name.

1. Find a pair of neighbouring countries whose names both begin with Z. (This is an easy one to get you started, as the only two countries in the world beginning with Z just happen to be neighbours.)

2. Find a pair of neighbouring countries whose names both begin with I. (A little more challenging; eight countries have I as their first letter.)

3. Find a pair of neighbouring countries whose names both begin with L. (These two nations also use a common currency and are virtually identical in physical size, give or take 1%.)

4. Find a pair of neighbouring countries whose names both begin with M. (There are two possible answers here.)

5. Find a pair of neighbouring countries whose names both begin with N. (In fact, these countries share not just one initial but their first *five* letters. The reason they have such similar designations is because they are named after the same river, which flows through both nations.)

6. Find a pair of neighbouring countries whose names both begin with E. (From the 1950s, they were one country, but it was an uncomfortable union for these historic adversaries and they split four decades later.)

7. Find a pair of neighbouring countries whose names both begin with K. (Although one is more than a dozen times larger than the other, they are close allies with very similar language, culture and religion.)

8. Find a pair of neighbouring countries whose names both begin with B. (Again, there are two possible answers, from different continents.)

9. Find a pair of neighbouring countries whose names both begin with A. (These two maintain no diplomatic relations. They have fought multiple wars and as a consequence their common border is heavily militarised.)

10. And, for the final question, a *trio*! Find a group of three countries – each of which borders the other two – and whose names all begin with C.

76 LANDMARKS OF THE EAST
Answers on page 207

Identify the famous sights depicted below and connect each one to its correct location on the map.

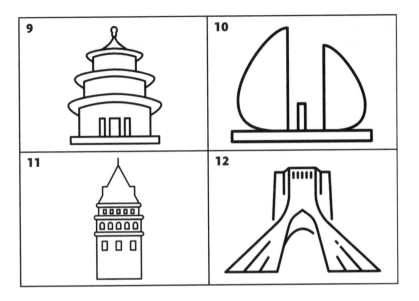

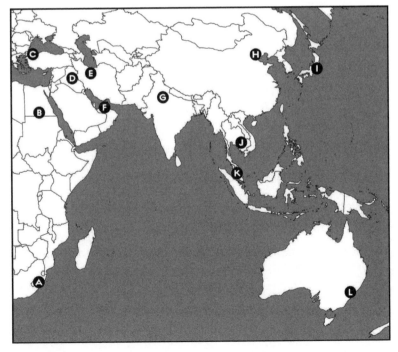

77 RIGHT ON THE MONEY
Answers on page 207

1. What was the currency used in Germany until it adopted the Euro in 2002?

2. What nickname is often used for the Canadian $1 coin, in reference to the bird depicted on most versions minted since 1987?

3. Which of these EU countries does *not* use the euro? Austria, Belgium, Czech Republic, Italy, Portugal, Slovakia.

4. Which of the world's present-day currencies has been in continuous circulation for the longest time, dating back to AD785?

5. What is the name of the currencies of both Zambia and Malawi?

6. Jordan, Serbia, Algeria, Tunisia and Bahrain are all among countries with currencies called what?

7. AUD is the official code for the currency of which country?

8. What country uses a currency called 'dong'?

9. Name one of the five countries with a currency called 'shilling'.

10. Which country uses a currency with the same name as that used in Italy until 2002?

11. North and South Korea use currencies with what name?

12. The real – plural reais – is the currency of which country?

13. The British pound is the world's fourth most traded currency after the euro, US dollar and which other?

14. The currency of which of these countries is not called 'dollars'? Australia, Belize, Fiji, Malaysia, Suriname.

15. Prior to the euro, escudos were used as the currency in Portugal. Which other country still uses a currency by that name?

16. The symbol ₹ was adopted in 2010 as the official sign for which currency? Prior to this, 'Rs' was the usual abbreviated form.

17. The ¥ sign is the international symbol used for the currencies of Japan and which other Asian country?

18. What is the name for the currency of Thailand?

19. Which country uses the zloty (meaning 'golden'), which is subdivided into 100 grosz?

20. What do the currencies of Egypt, Lebanon, Sudan, South Sudan and Syria have in common with that of the United Kingdom?

21. Four South American countries use currencies with what name, literally meaning 'weight'?

22. What is the official currency of Vatican City?

23. The world's highest denomination banknote ever circulated – the 100 quintillion (100,000,000,000,000,000,000) pengő note – was issued in which country in 1946? (They also printed one with a denomination ten times larger still but, overtaken by inflation, it was never issued.)

24. Offering greater security and durability, banknotes printed on synthetic polymers are gradually gaining popularity worldwide. In 1988, which country became the first to issue such plastic notes?

25. Whose image has appeared on the currency of no fewer than 35 countries?

78 ALL ROADS LEAD TO ROME
Answers on page 207

1. What is the name of Italy's national airline?

2. Which of these is *not* a region of Italy? Abruzzo, Emilia-Romagna, Galicia, Lombardia, Puglia.

3. On Italian restaurant menus, what are 'antipasti'?

4. The land border of northern Italy is shared with four countries: France, Switzerland, Slovenia and which other?

5. Who painted the frescoes *The Creation of Adam* and *The Last Judgment* in the Sistine Chapel of the Apostolic Palace in Vatican City?

6. Which of these is Italy *not* credited with first inventing? The moped, Nutella spread, the parachute, the typewriter, the violin.

7. Two countries are enclaves of Italy: Vatican City and which other?

8. What is the name of Rome's largest Baroque fountain, into which more than €1 million worth of coins are thrown annually by wish-makers?

9. The so-called 'industrial triangle' of northern Italy is formed by the cities of Milan, Turin and which other?

10. Which of these is *not* a type of Italian pasta? Conchiglie, farfalle, fettuccine, mazzanti, radiatori.

11. What is the English name for Rome's monumental stairway, known in Italian as the Scalinata di Trinità dei Monti, that climbs up from Piazza di Spagna to the Trinità dei Monti church?

12. Who was the prime minister of Italy 2001–06 and again 2008–11?

13. Which Italian city has been known as 'La Serenissima' and 'Queen of the Adriatic', among other terms?

14. Which of these is *not* an Italian cheese? Gorgonzola, mascarpone, parmesan, ricotta, telemea.

15. Which of these Italian cities is furthest south? Bologna, Naples, Palermo, Pisa, Rome, Venice.

79 HIGH AND MIGHTY
Answers on page 208

In the grid below, find the names of 20 mountains or mountain ranges of the world. Words may run forwards or backwards in a vertical, horizontal or diagonal direction.

E	I	G	E	R	O	B	S	O	N
T	A	E	K	A	N	U	A	M	A
N	T	N	T	A	L	I	A	S	T
A	L	L	R	U	J	K	L	N	I
H	A	U	D	U	A	S	P	O	P
S	J	A	F	L	P	L	S	W	A
N	G	S	U	R	U	A	T	D	C
E	L	B	R	U	S	R	N	O	L
I	O	L	Y	M	P	U	S	N	E
T	S	E	N	I	N	N	E	P	A

80 DEAR OLD BLIGHTY
Answers on page 208

1. What is the name of London's famous botanical garden, founded in 1840 and housing the world's largest and most diverse plant collections?

2. What is the short name for the London Orbital Motorway which runs in a 188km (117-mile) ring around the British capital city?

3. The name of the Welsh town of Llanfairpwllgwyngyllgogerychwyrn-drobwllllantysiliogogogoch is second-longest of any place in the world (after New Zealand's Taumatawhakatangihangakoauauotamateaturi-pukakapikimaungahoronukupokaiwhenuakitanatahu). On what island in Wales is this town located?

4. What do the English towns of Leamington Spa, Tunbridge Wells and Wootton Bassett have in common?

5. The UK's national flag is a juxtaposition of the flags of three of its four constituent countries. Which one is missing?

6. Which of these is not an official role held by the British monarch? UK head of state; commander-in-chief of the British Armed Forces; head of the Commonwealth; head of the Church of England; Lord High Chancellor of Great Britain.

7. 'Great Britain' is not synonymous with the 'United Kingdom'. What's the key difference in meaning between these two terms?

8. Said to be the oldest military ceremony in the world – possibly dating back as far as the 14th century – the Ceremony of the Keys takes place at 9:53pm every evening at which historic British building?

9. Which of these bizarre-sounding festivals is not a genuine annual event held in the UK? World's Biggest Liar Contest; World Worm-Charming Championships; Hereford Cow-Painting Festival; Cooper's Hill Cheese-Rolling; World Bog Snorkelling Championships.

10. The floral emblems of England, Wales and Northern Ireland are the rose, leek (or daffodil) and shamrock respectively. What is Scotland's corresponding national flower?

11. In which English town would you find William Shakespeare's birthplace?

12. Which of these places in Scotland is furthest north? Aberdeen, Dundee, Edinburgh, Glasgow, Inverness.

13. What is the name of the University of Oxford's main research library? It is one of the oldest libraries in Europe and counts among its buildings the circular Radcliffe Camera, one of Oxford's most famous sights.

14. Located on the northwestern outskirts of London, what is the name of the largest stadium in the UK, home to the English national football team as well as the headquarters of the Football Association?

15. Several London streets have become famous for particular trades. What profession is associated with Harley Street?

16. What profession is associated with Fleet Street?

17. And what profession is associated with Saville Row?

18. Which of these cities is closest to Birmingham by the most direct road route? Cambridge, Cardiff, Liverpool, London, Manchester.

19. Writer Frederic Raphael coined the tongue-in-cheek nickname 'city of perspiring dreams' in reference to Cambridge as a play on which well-known poetic description of rival university city Oxford?

20. By what name is the parliament building of Northern Ireland commonly known?

21. What is the most populous city in Scotland?

22. Who is the patron saint of Wales?

23. The traditional British breakfast dish called 'bubble and squeak' is made principally with potatoes and what other vegetable?

24. Who was the previous British monarch before Queen Elizabeth II?

25. In the Harry Potter books written by J K Rowling, the Hogwarts School of Witchcraft and Wizardry is accessed by travelling on the *Hogwarts Express* from King's Cross station in London, but this magical train cannot be boarded from the regular Muggle platforms at the station. What is the platform number for the train to Hogwarts?

81 COME RAIN OR SHINE
Answers on page 208

This quiz is about weather phenomena and natural disasters worldwide.

1. Which of these European cities receives the highest annual rainfall, on average? Glasgow, Lisbon, London, Milan, Paris, Zurich.

2. And which of them receives the lowest annual rainfall?

3. Which Overseas Department of France holds the world records for the most rainfall in 12, 24, 72 and 96 hours?

4. What are the Chinook, Khamsin, Mistral, Pampero and Sirocco?

5. In which one of these cities does the sun rise every day of the year? Murmansk, Norilsk, Tromsø, Trondheim, Utqiagvik.

6. Everyone has heard of the *aurora borealis*, or 'northern lights', but what is the name for the 'southern lights', their equally impressive (albeit somewhat less accessible) Antarctic counterparts?

7. Swedish astronomer Anders Celsius developed a temperature scale based on the freezing and boiling points of water. Prior to 1743, in what critical way did his scale differ from the Celsius scale we use today?

8. Which of these cities is the sunniest (most hours of sunshine per year, on average)? Addis Ababa, Athens, Mexico City, Tel Aviv, Tokyo.

9. And which of them is the least sunny?

10. Approximately how many lightning strikes happen across the world in a typical hour? 16; 160; 1,600; 16,000 or 160,000?

11. Earthquake monitoring authorities nowadays use the more accurate Moment Magnitude Scale (MMS) to measure seismic activity, but what is the name of the rough-and-ready earthquake intensity measure, developed in the 1930s, that is still preferred by the news media?

12. Devised in 1805 by the Irish hydrographer and Royal Navy officer after whom it is named, what is the measuring system that relates wind speed to observed conditions?

13. Which of these cities is the warmest (average daily high across the whole year)? Baghdad, Darwin, Marrakesh, Nairobi, Riyadh.

14. And which of them is the coolest, on average?

15. What word deriving from the Arabic word for 'season' (probably via Portuguese and Dutch) refers to a seasonally reversing wind accompanied by marked changes in levels of precipitation?

16. A name for a weather phenomenon deriving from the Arabic word for 'blowing', what type of wind is a haboob?

17. The 1823 poem *Twas the Night Before Christmas* is credited with introducing the notion that Santa's sleigh is pulled by a team of reindeer. It mentions two of them as being named 'Dunder and Blixem' – the Dutch words for what pair of weather phenomena?

18. What caused catastrophic damage in the Haitian capital Port-au-Prince, including to the city's cathedral and National Palace, in 2010?

19. What phenomenon was responsible for at least 41 fatalities in the Van province of southeast Turkey on 4–5 February 2020?

20. What type of disaster resulted in an eye-watering US$46 billion of damage in Thailand in 2011? It disrupted manufacturing supply chains, notably causing a year-long global shortage of computer hard disks.

21. What catastrophe occurred in January 2019 in Brumadinho, Brazil, with the loss of 270 lives, making it the deadliest such disaster in the world since the 1970s?

22. In 1999, what natural disaster caused extensive damage in Sydney, Australia, with the cost of repairs well in excess of A$2 billion?

23. Known as a 'cyclone' in the southern hemisphere and as a 'hurricane' in the Atlantic and northeast Pacific regions, what is this weather phenomenon usually called when it occurs in the northwest Pacific?

24. In 2005, Hurricane Katrina caused US$125 billion in damage, making it the costliest ever. In which US state did it make landfall?

25. On what date in 2004 did the deadliest tsunami in recorded history occur, affecting several countries in the Indian Ocean region?

82 GONE WALKABOUT
Answers on page 208

Match each of these well-known Australian places with the locations marked A–L on the map below.

1. Adelaide

2. Alice Springs

3. Brisbane

4. Cairns

5. Canberra

6. Darwin

7. Fraser Island

8. Hobart

9. Kangaroo Island

10. Melbourne

11. Perth

12. Sydney

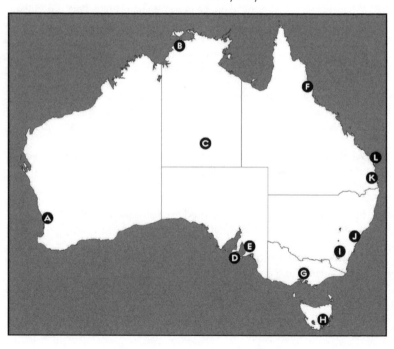

83 FAIR AND SQUARE
Answers on page 208

Across continents and cultures, city squares are a common feature of urban settlements, hosting festivals, markets, political rallies and protests. Test your knowledge of some of the world's best known of these popular meeting places for locals, tourists and pigeons alike.

1. Every two years, for a few days in August, Grand Place in Brussels is carpeted with a gigantic colourful design made from almost a million what?

2. Which square exhibits a rolling display of special artistic commissions atop a plinth initially erected in 1840 for a proposed king-on-horseback statue that never came to fruition? It finally hosted an equestrian sculpture of sorts 172 years later when, in 2012, the eighth temporary artwork to be shown there depicted a child on a rocking horse!

3. Seven of the world's 20 largest city squares are in which country?

4. In which famous square would you find Lenin's Mausoleum?

5. What is the name of the large plaza in Vatican City, designed around an ancient Egyptian obelisk that had been erected there in 1586?

6. Which bustling junction was known as Longacre Square until 1905 when it was it was renamed in honour of a 25-storey newspaper headquarters built there?

7. Alexanderplatz, named after Tsar Alexander I, is the second-largest square in Europe – but at the heart of which city is it located?

8. What is the name of the long, sloping square overlooked by the Czech National Museum in Prague?

9. In which city would you find the Millennium Memorial and a column topped by a statue of the Archangel Gabriel in Heroes' Square?

10. Plaza Bolívar is which capital city's main square, located in its La Candelaria district and home to the Palace of Justice, Lievano Palace, the National Capitol and the city's primary cathedral?

84 WINDMILLS OF YOUR MIND
Answers on page 208

Enter the answers to the numbered clues into the spiral grid, from the outside inwards. Each answer shares its final letter with the first letter of the next answer. The boxes for the first and last letters of each answer (where the answers overlap) are shaded grey.

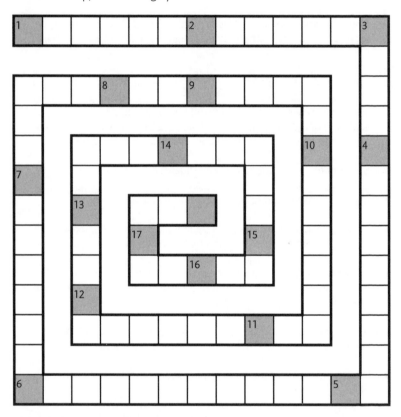

Once you have completed the spiral, rearrange the letters from the 18 shaded boxes to find the name of a semiaquatic animal.

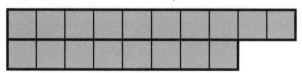

The number of letters in each answer is given in brackets after the clue.

1. An island nation famed for its volcanoes, huge glaciers and geysers (7)

2. The country where the Carlsberg beer, Bang & Olufsen electronics, ECCO shoes and Pandora jewellery brands are all headquartered (7)

3. The capital of Afghanistan since almost 250 years ago (5)

4. Descriptive of a country with no coastline (10)

5. An autocratic or despotic state (12)

6. A former French president after whom was named a famously inside-out building in Paris that houses the Public Information Library and National Museum of Modern Art (8)

7. The country whose largest cities are Montevideo and Salto (7)

8. A portable circular tent-like dwelling, covered with skins, inhabited by various nomadic groups in the steppes of Central Asia (4)

9. A ship which sank in 1912 on her maiden voyage from Southampton (7)

10. A species of penguin with a circumpolar distribution, named for the fine black line below its eyes and beak (9)

11. The country containing Europe's westernmost point (8)

12. A former French protectorate situated at the heart of the Indochinese peninsula (4)

13. An ancient settlement and capital of North Macedonia (6)

14. The EU Agency for Law Enforcement Cooperation (7)

15. The Peruvian capital city, with a population of 9 million (4)

16. A member of a Semitic people inhabiting much of the Middle East and North Africa (4)

17. The capital of Azerbaijan and the largest city on the Caspian Sea (4)

85 LIKE HERDING CATS
Answers on page 209

If the popularity of the Big Cat Festivals run by Bradt Travel Guides in London in recent years is any indication, big cats are among the number one species topping the bucket lists of a large proportion of wildlife travel fans. But how much do you know about where they live?

Match each of the cat species below with the corresponding distribution map showing its approximate range in the wild.

1. Cheetah

2. Jaguar

3. Leopard

4. Lion

5. Lynx (technically a group of four closely related species, including that widely known as the bobcat)

6. Puma (also known as the cougar or mountain lion)

7. Snow leopard (also known as the ounce)

8. Tiger

You will notice that panthers are not included on this list. That's because the word 'panther' refers not to one species but to any all-black big cat, usually leopards or jaguars. Roughly 10% of individuals of these species are melanistic. Until recent decades, there was widespread confusion over whether black panthers represented a separate species or not. The terminology is further complicated by the fact that, in scientific nomenclature, *Panthera* is the name of the genus that includes all lions, tigers, jaguars, leopards and snow leopards!

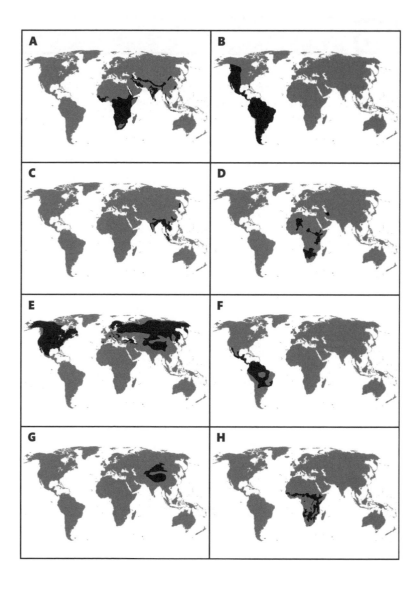

86 IRRITABLE VOWEL SYNDROME
Answers on page 209

An inexplicable mishap at the Bradt Guides printing presses has resulted in all the vowels being deleted from the names of some capital cities! Can you help us put things right by deciphering what each one should say?

1. RYKJVK

2. LNDN

3. RM

4. CNBRR

5. CR

6. TLLNN

7. DH

8. NRB

9. NKR

10. NTNNRV

11. SNTG

12. SLMBD

13. THRN

14. SL

15. THNS

16. TTW

17. P

18. GDG

87 JOY TO THE WORLD
Answers on page 209

1. The tradition of Christmas trees is thought to have originated in which country, where they are known as Weihnachtsbäume or Tannenbäume?

2. In the traditional carol *The Twelve Days of Christmas* – which was first published in England in 1780 but probably derives from an earlier French song – what gift is sent on the seventh day of Christmas?

3. Each December, a spruce of at least 20m (65 ft) is erected as a Christmas tree in London's Trafalgar Square – a gift from the capital city of which nation, as a token of gratitude for British support during World War II?

4. Which demonic horned figure from Central European folklore punishes naughty children at Christmas, in contrast to Saint Nicholas, who rewards the well-behaved with gifts?

5. What is Christmas called in France?

6. Santa Claus's name is a corruption of 'St Nicholas' (via Dutch 'Sinterklaas'). In which modern-day country was the real St Nicholas of Myra born, around AD270?

7. The melody of which popular Christmas carol is adapted from a piece of music written by Felix Mendelssohn to mark the 400th anniversary of Gutenberg's printing press?

8. On the day after Christmas and on New Year's Day, the streets of the Bahamas and many other English-speaking Caribbean nations come alive with flamboyant African-themed parades. The celebrations feature colourful costumes, music, and dancing to the beat of goatskin drums and cowbells. What are these festivals called?

9. In Finland, the name for Father Christmas is Joulupukki, from the Finnish words 'joulu' (yule) and 'pukki'. What kind of animal is a pukki? In neighbouring Sweden, representations of this same animal are traditionally made from straw as Christmas decorations.

10. In the year AD935, at the age of just 24, Václav I, Duke of Bohemia, was assassinated in a plot arranged by his younger brother, Boleslaus the Cruel. The duke was considered a martyr and immediately sainted. In which popular Christmas carol is he immortalised?

88 ARMCHAIR TRAVELLER
Answers on page 209

How well read are you? Match each of the ten synopses below with the name of the corresponding travel writer from the list opposite and, for a bonus point, identify the title of each book being described.

1. This 1957 classic of American literary counterculture chronicles a series of frenetic trips by the narrator and his Beat Generation friends. Set in the years after World War II, a combination of bus trips and daring hitchhiking takes these free-spirited adventurers on a journey across the USA against a backdrop of sex, drugs and jazz.

2. A drunken bet led to a month-long hitchhiking adventure with an unusual and cumbersome item of luggage in tow. The story of the whole ridiculous affair is told in this entertaining book, published in 1997.

3. This is the tale of the author's single-handed circumnavigation of Britain in a restored two-masted sailing boat, the *Gosfield Maid*, interspersed with flashbacks to a childhood with a vicar for a father. The journey happens to coincide with the Falklands War, and seamlessly woven into the narrative is a keenly perceptive portrait of Thatcher's Britain at this contentious moment in the country's political history.

4. First published in 1977, this influential travelogue was an original take on the age-old adventure tale. It has an unusual roving structure of 97 chapters, some just a paragraph long. The exhilarating narrative tells of the author's journey through South America in search of a mysterious ancient creature and the strange encounters had along the way.

5. This book could almost be viewed as a biography – its subject: the magical city of Venice. It is a masterfully written personal evocation of her architecture, her famous waterways, the character of her inhabitants, her sights and sounds, all set in historical context. The author had been smitten with the city for 15 years by the time this comprehensive portrait of Venetian life was first published in 1960.

6. An iconic travelogue, this 1958 tale follows a London fashion executive who, yearning for adventure, ropes a friend into coming along for a mountain-climbing adventure in Afghanistan. This witty and charming book recounts their exploits amid fascinating peoples and landscapes, as it transpires how woefully ill prepared they are for their challenge.

7.   Based on the author's daily diaries, this book documents a daring
1960s cycling trip through nine countries. Braving difficult mountainous
terrain, harsh winter conditions, hungry wolves and gangs of thieves, the
author pedals on with indomitable spirit across the Middle East – pistol
on hip – before eventually finishing up this epic journey in India.

8.   A humorous jaunt around some of the quirkier corners of the UK, this
book was penned by an unapologetic Anglophile who had made the
country his home for almost two decades. In the mid-nineties, having
resolved to move back to his native United States, the author sets out on
a valedictory tour of his adopted homeland, completing the trip almost
entirely by public transport.

9.   This '70s railway odyssey recounts the author's epic four-month journey
from London to the Middle East, across the Indian subcontinent and
through Southeast Asia, returning via the Trans-Siberian Railway. It
features several legendary rail routes but the real stars of the show are
neither the trains nor even the famous cities they connect: above all,
the narrative is concerned with the author's fellow travellers, who are
brought to life through the conversations struck up along the way.

10. In this memoir, the author embarks upon a trip in pursuit of worldly
pleasure and spiritual devotion, following a bitter divorce and a
turbulent affair. The ensuing voyage of self-discovery takes the reader
on a journey first to Italy, then India and finally Indonesia. Published in
2006, it remained on The *New York Times* Best Seller list for 187 weeks.

List of authors:

A. Bill Bryson   **F.** Jan Morris

B. Bruce Chatwin   **G.** Dervla Murphy

C. Elizabeth Gilbert   **H.** Eric Newby

D. Tony Hawks   **I.**   Jonathan Raban

E. Jack Kerouac   **J.**   Paul Theroux

89 STAN-DING OUT FROM THE CROWD
Answers on page 209

Bradt Travel Guides has a reputation for publishing pioneering guidebooks to unusual and out-of-the-way destinations. Among the least-known regions of the world are the 'Five Stans' located between China and the Caspian Sea – Kazakhstan, Kyrgyzstan, Tajikistan, Turkmenistan and Uzbekistan – and indeed Bradt is the only mainstream travel publisher to have released dedicated guides to all of them.

You do not need any information besides the clues below. Can you figure out each country's area, capital city, and who wrote the corresponding Bradt guidebook? Complete the table using the logic grid to help you (by marking positive and negative relationships with ticks and crosses respectively). Each option in each category appears exactly once in the solution.

1. The eight-letter name of Uzbekistan's capital ends with the same letter that it starts with.

2. The city of Dushanbe is located in the smallest of these five countries.

3. Ashgabat is the capital city of a country that Paul Brummell knows well, having been based there as British Ambassador between 2002 and 2005. He is the sole author of the Bradt guidebook to that country, which is between 250,000km² and 2,500,000km² in area.

4. Travel writer and linguist Maria Oleynik collaborated with Brummell on the latest edition of the guide with a chapter on Nur-Sultan. She was not involved in writing about any country beginning with T.

6. Uzbekistan is neither the largest nor even the second-largest country.

7. Sophie Ibbotson and Max Lovell-Hoare are renowned experts on this region. They have led numerous trips there, worked as government advisors on tourism, and co-authored Bradt's guide to Tajikistan.

8. Sophie Ibbotson also wrote a book about a country that is not 200,000km² in area – collaborating on the latest edition with veteran Bradt author Tim Burford, who specialises in post-Soviet nations.

9. The Kyrgyzstan guide was penned by esteemed travel writer and photographer Laurence Mitchell, who has a particular fascination with forgotten places, border zones and territories in transition.

10. Residents of Bishkek do not live in Tajikistan, and residents of Nur-Sultan do not live in the second-smallest country of the group.

		Bradt author					Capital city					Area				
		Brummell	Brummell & Oleynik	Ibbotson & Burford	Ibbotson & Lovell-Hoare	Mitchell	Ashgabat	Bishkek	Dushanbe	Nur-Sultan	Tashkent	143,000km²	200,000km²	448,000km²	491,000km²	2,725,000km²
Country	Kazakhstan															
	Kyrgyzstan															
	Tajikistan															
	Turkmenistan															
	Uzbekistan															
Area	143,000km²															
	200,000km²															
	448,000km²															
	491,000km²															
	2,725,000km²															
Capital city	Ashgabat															
	Bishkek															
	Dushanbe															
	Nur-Sultan															
	Tashkent															

Country	Bradt author	Capital city	Area
Kazakhstan			
Kyrgyzstan			
Tajikistan			
Turkmenistan			
Uzbekistan			

90 FICKLE FINGER OF FATE
Answers on page 209

The answers to all of these general knowledge questions begin with 'F'.

1. Typically accompanied by guitar music, what is the traditional southern Spanish form of song and dance often performed with castanets?

2. Which country borders Sweden, Norway and Russia?

3. Which autonomous archipelago within the Kingdom of Denmark is located in the North Atlantic between the Shetlands and Iceland?

4. Charles de Gaulle was president of which country from 1959 to 1969?

5. By what two-word name is the United States Bullion Depository in Kentucky more widely known?

6. What is the complex in central Beijing that houses the Palace Museum?

7. The words 'rain', 'montane' and 'boreal' can each precede what six-letter word to describe different types of habitat around the world?

8. What is the capital of the Australian territory of Christmas Island?

9. George Washington, Benjamin Franklin, Thomas Jefferson and John Adams are among a group collectively known by what alliterative term?

10. What is the dialect of Dutch spoken by over half of people in Belgium?

11. Which Colombian forward nicknamed 'El Tigre' has played for Porto, Atlético Madrid, Monaco and, from 2019, Galatasaray?

12. What is the name of Switzerland's currency?

13. What cocktail, created in 1915 by Paris barman Harry MacElhone, comprises champagne, lemon juice and sugar served in a flute glass?

14. The name of which country has four letters and three tittles?

15. Which guidebook imprint was acquired by Bradt Travel Guides in 2019, bringing together the UK's two largest independent travel publishers?

91 A FLYING START
Answers on page 209

Match these international airports with the locations they serve:

1.	Ben Gurion Airport	Amsterdam, Netherlands
2.	Charles de Gaulle Airport	Bogotá, Colombia
3.	David the Builder International Airport	Casablanca, Morocco
4.	El Dorado International Airport	Chicago, USA
5.	Gatwick Airport	Durban, South Africa
6.	Incheon International Airport	Kraków, Poland
7.	John Lennon Airport	Kutaisi, Georgia
8.	John Paul II International Airport	Liverpool, UK
9.	King Shaka International Airport	London, UK
10.	Marco Polo Airport	Moscow, Russia
11.	Mohammed V International Airport	Ontario, Canada
12.	O'Hare International Airport	Paris, France
13.	Schiphol Airport	Seoul, South Korea
14.	Thunder Bay International Airport	Tel Aviv, Israel
15.	Vnukovo International Airport	Venice, Italy

92 MOVERS AND SHAKERS
Answers on page 209

Identify each country from the trio of famous people born there. (In cases where country names or borders have since changed, we are looking for the present-day nation where you would find their birthplace.)

1.
- in 1707, father of plant and animal taxonomy Carl Linnaeus
- in 1833, Nobel Prizes founder and dynamite inventor Alfred Nobel
- in 1989, YouTuber and comedian, PewDiePie

2.
- around AD100, mathematician and astronomer Ptolemy
- in 1932, film and television actor Omar Sharif
- in 1933, businessman Mohamed Al-Fayed

3.
- around 1451, explorer and navigator Christopher Columbus
- in 1564, astronomer and physicist Galileo
- in 1934, screen actress Sophia Loren

4.
- in 1871, physicist and discoverer of alpha particles Ernest Rutherford
- in 1944, opera singer Kiri Te Kanawa
- in 1919, explorer and mountaineer Edmund Hillary

5.
- in 1805, prolific fairy-tale writer Hans Christian Andersen
- in 1885, quantum physicist Niels Bohr
- in 1990, top professional tennis player Caroline Wozniacki

6.
- in 1892, fantasy writer J R R Tolkien
- in 1971, technology entrepreneur Elon Musk
- in 1975, actress and producer Charlize Theron

7.
- in 1898, surrealist painter René Magritte
- in 1929, actress and humanitarian Audrey Hepburn
- in 1960, actor and martial artist Jean-Claude Van Damme

8.
- around 570BC, philosopher and triangle enthusiast Pythagoras
- in 1921, Duke of Edinburgh and husband of Elizabeth II, Prince Philip
- in 1962, heavy-metal and hard-rock drummer Tommy Lee

9.
- in 1810, composer and virtuoso pianist Frédéric Chopin
- in 1867, pioneering radioactivity scientist Marie Curie
- in 1877, beautician and entrepreneur Max Factor

10. · in 1940, legendary footballer Pelé
· in 1947, lyricist and novelist Paulo Coelho
· in 1960, Formula One racing driver Ayrton Senna

11. · in 1856, neurologist and psychoanalyst Sigmund Freud
· in 1883, novelist Franz Kafka
· in 1956, tennis champion Martina Navrátilová

12. · in 1898, prime minister of Israel (1969–74) Golda Meir
· in 1923, media mogul, politician and fraudster Robert Maxwell
· in 1983, television and film actress Mila Kunis

13. · in 1946, magician Uri Geller
· in 1949, rock star and television personality Gene Simmons
· in 1981, Star Wars actress Natalie Portman

14. · in 1903, comedian and entertainer Bob Hope
· in 1955, inventor of the World Wide Web, Tim Berners-Lee
· in 1977, television presenter Jerry Springer

15. · in 1907, surrealist portrait painter Frida Kahlo
· in 1966, film actress Salma Hayek
· in 1969, canine behaviourist and television presenter César Millán

16. · in 1955, cellist Yo-Yo Ma
· in 1946, wrestler and actor André the Giant
· in 1990, Harry Potter movie actress Emma Watson

17. · in 1946, Queen frontman Freddie Mercury
· in 1959, award-winning author Katherine Scholes
· in 1962, BBC journalist Alan Johnston

18. · in 1956, disgraced former parliamentarian Keith Vaz
· in 1962, stand-up comedian and political activist Eddie Izzard
· in 1997, rapper Ali Gatie

93 WORLD LEADERS

Answers on page 209

Across

7. Successor to François Mitterrand (7,6)

8. A thought, concept or belief (4)

9. Island where former Italian prime minister, and later president, Francesco Cossiga was born (8)

10. Roman, Persian or Ottoman sphere of influence, for instance (6)

12. An organised group with a purpose (4)

13. Initials of Turkish leader in power since 2003 (1,1,1)

14. Annual occurrence named in honour of Roman general Julius Caesar (4)

15. The 40th US president, in office 1981–89 (6)

16. Russian empresses or wives of autocratic rulers (8)

19. Australian prime minister in office 2007–10 and again in 2013 (4)

20. Descriptive of countries led by Hassan Rouhani, King Salman or Bashar al-Assad, for instance (6,7)

Down

1. President of Iraq who was in power for almost 24 years (6,7)

2. Ultimate goal of egalitarianism (8)

3. Hitler's Deputy during World War II (4)

4. Angela Merkel's predecessor (8)

5. Nickname of Israeli prime minister Benjamin Netanyahu (4)

6. Prime minister of New Zealand from 2017 (7,6)

11. Longest-serving Swedish prime minister (8)

12. Supporter of John Major's successor (8)

17. Prime minister of the Moldavian Soviet Socialist Republic in the 1940s and 1950s (4)

18. An emperor, king, prince or lord in Iran (4)

94 A HEAD FOR HEIGHTS
Answers on page 209

Match each lettered entity in the right-hand column with its height.
(The mountain peaks are measured by their elevation above sea level.)

1.	1.63m (5 ft 4 in)	**A.**	Eiffel Tower, Paris
2.	1.70m (5 ft 7 in)	**B.**	Mount Kilimanjaro, Tanzania
3.	1.78m (5 ft 10 in)	**C.**	The highest point in France
4.	1.88m (6 ft 2 in)	**D.**	Space Needle, Seattle
5.	2.40m (7 ft 10 in)	**E.**	Queen Elizabeth II
6.	5.80m (19 ft)	**F.**	Burj Khalifa, Dubai
7.	52m (169 ft)	**G.**	George, the world's tallest giraffe
8.	93m (305 ft)	**H.**	The highest point in the Maldives
9.	98m (322 ft)	**I.**	Xi Jinping, president of China
10.	184m (604 ft)	**J.**	Nelson's Column, London
11.	324m (1,063 ft)	**K.**	Vladimir Putin, president of Russia
12.	340m (1,115 ft)	**L.**	Mount Snowdon, Wales
13.	443m (1,454 ft)	**M.**	Peter the Great statue, Moscow
14.	553m (1,815 ft)	**N.**	Mount Hillaby, Barbados
15.	828m (2,717 ft)	**O.**	Empire State Building, New York
16.	1,085m (3,560 ft)	**P.**	Bill Clinton, former US president
17.	3,776m (12,388 ft)	**Q.**	CN Tower, Toronto
18.	4,810m (15,781 ft)	**R.**	Mount Fuji, Japan
19.	5,895m (19,341 ft)	**S.**	The highest point in Pakistan
20.	8,611m (28,251 ft)	**T.**	Statue of Liberty, New York

95 I'LL DRINK TO THAT!
Answers on page 210

1. Caipirinha is the national cocktail of which country?

2. Which nation consumes the most beer per capita, by far?

3. Cider is the official state beverage of New Hampshire and in Florida it is orange juice. What drink do Arkansas, New York and Pennsylvania share with more than a dozen other US states as *their* official beverage?

4. Which are the only two countries that can produce red-wine-based punch under the name of 'sangria' according to EU regulations?

5. Ouzo, rakı, sambuca and arak (from Greece, Turkey, Italy and the Middle East respectively) are liqueurs with what flavour in common?

6. Made with sweetened dried persimmon and ginger, sujeonggwa is a traditional cinnamon punch from which country?

7. In other languages, which of these is *not* used to mean 'cheers!' when raising your glass? Aiuto, gesondheid, na zdravi, prost, salud, santé, skål.

8. Each year, Americans drink 91 litres of Coca-Cola, equivalent to 278 regular cans. Which is the only country to consume more per capita, with a considerably higher average consumption equal to 513 cans?

9. Brennivín (literally 'burning wine') is a clear schnapps considered to be the signature distilled beverage of which nation?

10. The Cuban capital of Havana is famously the birthplace of which rum-based cocktail made with lime juice, soda water and mint?

11. Which country is the soft drink Lemon & Paeroa (known as L&P) from?

12. Popular in Eastern Europe and the Middle East, ayran (or doogh) is made by watering down what with chilled water and adding salt?

13. Which gin-based drink is traditionally associated with the UK's Wimbledon tennis tournament and the Henley Royal Regatta?

14. Which country is the origin of the cream liqueur called Amarula, which is made from sugar, cream and the fruit of the marula tree?

96 NEW WORLD ORDER
Answers on page 210

Match each of these South American countries with those marked A–H on the map opposite.

1. Argentina

2. Brazil

3. Chile

4. Ecuador

5. Guyana

6. Peru

7. Uruguay

8. Venezuela

Match these cities, islands and popular tourist destinations with the places marked I–V.

9. Angel Falls

10. Asunción

11. Bogotá

12. Brasília

13. Caracas

14. Falkland Islands

15. Galápagos Islands

16. Lake Titicaca

17. Machu Picchu

18. Montevideo

19. Santiago

20. South Georgia Island

21. Trinidad and Tobago

22. Uyuni Salt Flat

Match these rivers with those marked W–Z.

23. Amazon River

24. Iguazu River

25. Orinoco River

26. Paraguay River

97 BARKING UP THE WRONG TREE
Answers on page 210

1. In popular culture, Robin Hood and his band of merry men are portrayed as living in which British forest?

2. What type of leaf is featured on the Canadian flag?

3. Dating back more than a thousand years, bonsai is the practice of cultivating miniature trees in a form that mimics the shape of their full-size cousins. In which country did this art form develop?

4. Which one of these does not grow on trees? Avocados, cocoa beans, lychees, mangos, pineapples, pomegranates.

5. Which country contains the largest part of the Amazon rainforest?

6. By what name is the tree *Araucaria araucana* known, in reference to the purported difficulty primates have in climbing it? Although native to Chile and Argentina, it is now widely grown around the world.

7. Which forested mountainous region of southwest Germany is known locally as der Schwarzwald?

8. There are eight species of baobab trees. All but two of them are native to which country?

9. *Quercus* is the scientific name for which genus of trees that grow predominantly throughout the northern hemisphere?

10. Which one of these products does not come from trees? Camphor, cinnamon, cork, cotton, loofah/luffa sponges, rubber.

11. Which country has the largest area of forest cover in the world – over 8 million square kilometres?

12. Towering up to 116m (380 ft) in height, Hyperion is the world's tallest tree. It stands in a national park in northern California and researchers believe it might have been even taller were it not for woodpecker damage at the top. What type of tree is Hyperion?

13. Resin harvested from pine trees is distilled to make what solvent, widely used in paints and varnishes?

14. Teak (*Tectona grandis*) is a hardwood tree species native to which continent?

15. Eucalyptus trees are a group of some 700 species, most of which are native to Australia, where their leaves are eaten by koalas. By what three-letter name do Australians commonly call this kind of tree?

16. *A Thousand Trees* is a song from the debut album of which Welsh rock band, released in 1997?

17. Sometimes known as the maidenhair tree, *Ginkgo biloba* is the sole surviving representative of an entire evolutionary branch of trees that date back to the Triassic period. Which country is it native to?

18. Which one of these does not grow on trees? Almonds, brazil nuts, cashew nuts, peanuts, pistachio nuts, walnuts.

19. Argan oil, produced from the kernels of the argan tree (*Argania spinosa*), is an increasingly popular ingredient in cosmetics such as lip gloss, shampoo, moisturisers and soaps. The tree is endemic to which country, where its oil is used as a dip for bread at breakfast time?

20. Which is the only country in the world named after a tree?

21. What is the common name of the *Ochroma pyramidale* tree, native to Central and South America, which yields a lightweight timber often used in table tennis bats, wind turbine blades, fishing lures and surfboards?

22. The flag of which country consists of a green cedar tree on a background of three red and white bands?

23. In Britain and some parts of North America, the nuts of which trees are used in the traditional children's playground game of conkers?

24. Which of these is the scientific study of trees? Astacology, campanology, deltiology, dendrology, selenology, trichology.

25. What is the name of the otherworldly mushroom-shaped trees native to the Yemeni archipelago of Socotra? Since the 18th century, the tree's red sap has been used as a source of varnish for violins.

98 NAPA VALLEY
Answers on page 210

Shade only the boxes containing letters that appear in 'Napa Valley' to reveal an image depicting the perfect way to see this beautiful wine-growing region of California.

Z	M	Q	I	S	J	S	J	I	D	G	B	N	E	N	P	L	N	C	Q	M	Z	M	H	T	S	D	K	B	S
I	S	D	G	I	X	U	F	Q	V	E	P	V	V	Y	V	A	E	N	A	L	T	G	K	S	C	T	F	R	B
K	T	I	X	O	S	R	L	P	E	W	G	I	N	N	V	P	J	I	I	Y	N	A	B	Q	S	R	G	Z	U
S	O	X	M	F	P	Y	L	P	I	F	W	N	E	A	E	N	P	C	R	D	E	P	P	A	U	G	D	J	T
D	D	B	Z	N	E	V	Y	W	J	U	Z	P	N	L	Y	Y	P	Q	H	O	U	L	V	E	L	I	I	J	U
W	C	R	V	Y	Y	V	Q	H	W	J	Q	V	Y	P	Y	A	A	U	R	W	D	U	L	L	L	P	W	D	C
B	B	L	L	A	Y	A	U	T	W	Z	Y	L	L	A	N	A	N	E	T	R	J	B	L	Y	P	Y	A	J	H
Q	Y	V	E	L	E	B	Z	F	M	D	L	L	A	L	V	A	E	Y	K	M	O	I	M	N	V	N	V	E	M
J	E	P	V	E	N	U	I	Z	H	U	P	A	P	A	L	V	N	L	U	D	H	Z	H	V	L	A	N	L	K
H	E	V	Y	V	A	Z	H	O	W	I	Y	V	N	P	Y	L	L	A	Q	K	Q	T	I	N	A	V	V	A	B
N	L	N	V	V	G	S	H	G	Q	C	L	L	N	L	V	V	E	P	X	X	G	Z	F	M	E	Y	P	Y	Y
E	V	P	N	Y	X	Q	W	M	G	D	E	P	A	L	P	P	N	Y	X	F	K	B	O	I	Y	P	P	A	E
P	V	L	V	N	G	D	W	M	X	S	V	L	V	E	P	Y	E	Y	R	X	S	D	W	W	E	Y	P	E	A
V	N	V	E	A	X	H	H	Q	I	I	E	L	A	P	N	Y	A	E	B	B	M	F	K	X	N	Y	N	A	L
Y	Y	L	A	A	H	O	S	D	T	H	A	L	A	V	L	L	V	N	S	H	Q	U	S	T	E	P	V	P	V
T	V	P	Y	V	Y	C	C	C	D	F	L	L	L	Y	L	N	P	L	V	G	R	X	F	F	E	A	L	E	L	Z
G	V	L	A	P	N	H	Z	W	G	H	V	A	P	Y	P	Y	N	V	B	D	T	F	C	N	Y	E	P	L	B
T	E	E	N	Y	A	M	Q	D	H	O	A	A	V	N	V	E	P	A	T	X	Q	Q	G	L	N	A	P	P	K
D	K	Y	P	A	N	F	M	D	B	F	V	Y	Y	N	A	A	A	P	G	G	F	Z	T	A	L	V	E	T	W
T	M	V	N	E	Y	N	C	G	R	U	L	A	V	P	A	N	E	Y	F	F	B	F	V	V	L	N	Y	K	Q
I	B	M	Y	P	E	V	O	U	G	J	I	V	Y	Y	L	N	Y	G	W	W	M	Q	E	E	A	A	O	I	I
M	U	U	Y	L	Y	P	P	D	X	J	M	N	N	N	P	E	P	H	F	X	X	Y	Y	L	P	L	I	W	J
I	S	T	G	N	A	E	N	X	M	O	K	P	Y	E	V	E	L	R	O	I	R	E	Y	E	P	M	B	R	R
C	S	H	Q	D	N	L	A	E	D	U	F	V	V	P	E	A	V	G	O	K	Y	A	N	Y	M	Z	C	M	K
C	I	D	Q	I	O	Y	E	P	O	Q	U	T	N	L	Y	Y	X	I	F	H	V	L	A	B	T	B	G	X	F
H	Z	B	C	S	Z	P	N	A	V	I	C	Z	L	A	N	V	U	H	Z	Y	N	V	Y	Q	Z	H	D	M	R
S	X	S	F	Q	B	R	A	P	A	K	Q	T	A	L	N	L	W	U	J	E	A	A	U	H	C	W	S	M	G
D	X	F	G	Z	M	R	H	E	P	N	F	I	E	P	N	A	R	J	Y	Y	P	C	O	B	R	O	X	X	D
B	Q	D	X	W	F	M	W	F	E	P	A	X	I	L	E	K	D	A	A	L	S	Q	M	K	O	K	X	W	K
K	H	S	S	G	Q	H	D	J	O	E	L	N	H	E	P	X	E	E	E	F	I	H	S	Z	T	H	F	C	O
O	F	B	T	H	M	Z	C	B	O	C	V	U	A	A	E	E	C	Y	T	I	T	X	H	O	I	X	S	S	F
M	R	B	H	C	S	C	H	I	I	H	N	K	U	X	H	D	S	V	G	R	X	B	X	R	F	O	W	R	R
O	I	O	H	S	I	S	Z	H	Z	G	J	N	J	T	H	I	P	Q	H	S	O	M	C	K	D	O	Q	Q	H
C	I	T	Z	H	K	W	C	I	Z	U	K	L	N	A	N	L	V	C	C	D	I	U	T	F	G	O	S	W	T
G	R	K	B	I	C	I	R	H	Z	B	Z	E	Y	A	E	L	A	R	Z	C	U	Q	D	T	I	D	H	U	T
H	R	D	B	K	Z	X	R	Q	J	G	H	E	P	N	E	L	L	Q	M	D	D	C	D	K	F	I	D	F	K
M	R	W	F	S	B	O	H	G	B	W	Q	Y	V	Y	E	V	L	I	R	C	C	Q	X	C	W	M	B	G	D

99 ODDBALLS
Answers on page 210

In each of the following lists, identify the odd one out and explain the reason why.

1. Alice Springs, Auckland, Brisbane, Cairns, Darwin, Hobart, Perth.

2. Austria, France, Germany, Hungary, Italy, Liechtenstein.

3. Australian flag, Chilean flag, Czech flag, Dutch flag, French flag, German flag, Russian flag, UK flag, US flag.

4. Bananaquit, hoary puffleg, masked booby, mountain chicken, great potoo, tawny frogmouth, shoebill.

5. Bahrain, Cuba, Iceland, Madagascar, Malta, Taiwan, Vietnam.

6. Abba, Greta Thunberg, Ikea, Minecraft, Nobel Prize in Literature, Nokia, Spotify, Volvo Cars.

7. Bilbao, Bilbster, Bilby, Bilsby, Bilsdon, Bilsham, Bilston, Bilting, Bilton.

8. Mustafa Kemal Atatürk, David Beckham, George H W Bush, Bob Hope, John F Kennedy, Imam Khomeini, John Lennon, Nikola Tesla, John Wayne.

9. Ghana, Ireland, Mali, Peru, Portugal, Senegal, United Kingdom.

10. Bombay duck, electric eel, flying fox, flying lemur, guinea pig, killer whale, king cobra, koala bear, maned wolf, polar bear, prairie dog, red panda.

11. Malawi, Michigan, Nicaragua, Ontario, Paris, Victoria.

12. Brazil, Ecuador, Gabon, India, Indonesia, Kenya, Somalia, Uganda.

13. Tiger, panda, whale, bull, lemon, goblin, Greenland.

14. Barbara, Carla, Eleanor, Hillary, Laura, Michelle, Nancy.

15. Bazantar, bougarabou, esraj, jiaohu, låtfiol, lirone, rebab, zhonghu.

16. Atlam, Esrever, Lagenes, Lapen, Nari, Nobag, Regin, Soal, Yawron.

100 ALPHABET SOUP

Answers on page 211

This quiz of worldwide general knowledge has answers from A to Z.

1. What A is a country whose flag comprises three horizontal bands: red, white and red?

2. What B is a country where salteñas are a popular national dish?

3. What C is a country bordering Libya?

4. What D is the river connecting the capital cities of Austria and Serbia?

5. What E is the river that, along with the Tigris, defines Mesopotamia?

6. What F is a type of cable-operated railway designed for ascending and descending very steep inclines?

7. What G is a country invaded by Russia in 2008?

8. What H is a strait between the Persian Gulf and the Gulf of Oman?

9. What I is a famous waterfall and river on the border between Brazil and Argentina?

10. What J is a country whose full title is the 'Hashemite Kingdom'?

11. What K is a flightless bird of New Zealand also known as an 'owl parrot'?

12. What L is the largest airline in Germany?

13. What M is a US state with a coastline on the Gulf of Mexico?

14. What N is the only country whose flag is neither square nor rectangular?

15. What O is the highest mountain in Greece?

16. What P is the city served by Charles de Gaulle Airport?

17. What Q is the only walled city north of Mexico?

18. What R is the currency of South Africa?

19. What S is a Canadian province?

20. What T is the country where you would be welcomed with the word 'hoşgeldiniz'?

21. What U is the local, and now preferred, name for Australia's Ayers Rock?

22. What V is a country with cities called Maracaibo, Barquisimeto and Caracas?

23. What W is New Zealand's third most populous city?

24. What X describes plants that can survive in extremely dry habitats?

25. What Y is the most-visited national park in California?

26. What Z is the main square in Mexico City?

101 ARABIAN NIGHTS
Answers on page 211

Match each of these Middle Eastern places with the locations marked A–L on the map below.

1. Baghdad

2. Damascus

3. Doha

4. Dubai

5. Isfahan

6. Jerusalem

7. Kuwait City

8. Mecca

9. Muscat

10. Riyadh

11. Socotra

12. Tehran

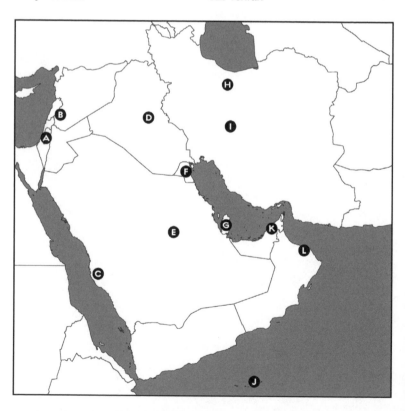

102 A ROOM WITH A VIEW
Answers on page 211

1. Named for the New York hotel where it was invented in 1896, which dish is nowadays typically made with celery, apples and mayonnaise – along with walnuts and grapes that were not part of the original recipe?

2. In which country would you find Giraffe Manor, situated in a giraffe sanctuary, where guests can feed the animals from their breakfast table?

3. Which seaside town was the setting for British television sitcom *Fawlty Towers*, featuring a terribly run hotel? It was based on a real hotel called Gleneagles, located in that same town until being demolished in 2016.

4. What is unusual about the world-famous hotel opened in 1990 in the Swedish village of Jukkasjärvi?

5. Under construction since 1987, the Ryugyong Hotel is a 105-storey pyramid-shaped skyscraper located in which country?

6. In which '70s hit did the Eagles sing of a place to stay where 'you can check out any time you like, but you can never leave'?

7. Martin Luther King Jr was assassinated on the balcony of The Lorraine Motel in which city in 1968?

8. In which country would you find the luxury colonial-style Raffles Hotel, where a famous gin-based sling cocktail was purportedly invented?

9. At Hotel Costa Verde, located in the forest at the edge of Costa Rica's Manuel Antonio National Park, what has been recycled into luxury accommodation?

10. Which hotel, situated off the Strand in London, is accessed by a short public road where cars are required to drive on the *right*?

11. In which 2011 movie, based on the novel *These Foolish Things* by Deborah Moggach, do a group of British pensioners move to a retirement hotel in India, run by the young and eager Sonny?

12. Michael Jackson caused outrage when, in the excitement of the moment, he dangled his infant son out of a hotel window in which city in 2002?

103 DEEP AND MEANINGFUL
Answers on page 211

The origins of some place names are lost in the mists of time but many others have documented etymologies. England, for instance, literally means 'land of the Angles' – the Angles being Germanic settlers who went on to found several Anglo-Saxon kingdoms.

1. 'Land of the Rising Sun' is a loose translation of the name of which Asian country?

2. Which nation is named in honour of Prince Philip of Asturias, who went on to become King Philip II of Spain?

3. Which country's name means 'the Saviour' in Spanish, being an abbreviated form of the phrase 'province of our Lord Jesus Christ, saviour of the world'?

4. The name of which Mediterranean island is often said to take its name from the local word for copper, a metal that was first mined there more than 5,000 years ago. In reality, the reverse is true: the metal is named after the island.

5. In the local Slavic language, which country's name means 'white Russian'?

6. Which nation bordering the Red Sea takes its name from the Ancient Greek word for 'red'?

7. The name of which country means 'little Venice' in Italian, after the native stilt houses reminded explorers Alonso de Ojeda and Amerigo Vespucci of Venice in 1499?

8. In the local Bambara language spoken by most people in Mali, what is the meaning of the word 'mali'?

9. Argentina was named in 1520 for a quality of La Plata River. What does it mean?

10. 'South' is the literal translation of which country's name, being a shortened form of the Latin phrase for 'unknown southern land'?

11. The names of the countries of Congo, India, Jordan, Moldova, Niger, Senegal and Uruguay have what in common, with regard to their origin?

12. Owing to its complex colonial history, the African nation of Cameroon takes its name from French 'Cameroun', in turn coming from German 'Kamerun', from the Anglicised 'Cameroons', which itself derived from Portuguese 'Camarões'! But what does the word mean?

13. Which European country's name derives from a Phoenician Punic word for the hyrax? This is a little odd, given that hyraxes don't live there, but it is likely that the word was mistakenly used in reference to the rabbits that do!

14. Canada takes its name from a native Iroquoian word – 'kanada' – but what does it mean?

15. Which nation's name is a corruption of the last part of the Arabic phrase 'Jazā'ir al-Qamar', meaning 'islands of the Moon'?

104 IT'S ALL GREEK TO ME

Answers on page 211

This quiz will test your knowledge of the glorious diversity of written languages that exist around the world.

1. In which country would you find the writing system shown on the right?

กรุงเทพมหานคร

2. Which post-Soviet country uses the alphabet in which this example sentence is written?

კეთილ მგზავრობას გისურვებთ

3. Which of these four writing samples labelled A–D is Japanese?

A.
도널드 트럼프

4. Which of them is Mandarin Chinese?

B.
ドナルド・トランプ

5. Which of them is Malayalam (spoken in the Indian state of Kerala and the union territories of Lakshadweep and Puducherry)?

C.
ഡോണൾഡ് ട്രംപ്

D.
唐纳德·特朗普

6. Which of them is Korean?

7. In what language is this sample of text written?

Ελληνικό αλφάβητο

8. Variations of which alphabet are used for writing languages that include Russian (as in the example shown), Belarussian, Ukrainian, Kyrgyz and Bulgarian?

Все счастливые семьи похожи друг на друга, каждая несчастливая семья несчастлива по-своему.

9. In which major language is this tricky tongue twister written?

روحي وروحك ياروحي روحين بروح, مطرح ما تروح روحك روحي بتروح

10. These are the numbers from one to ten written out in which language?

אחת שתים שלש ארבע חמש
שש שבע שמונה תשע עשר

11-18. Can you identify these eight famous people whose names have been transcribed or encoded into various alternative forms?

11. Леонардо Ди Каприо

12. Κιμ Καρντάσιαν

13. /ˈstiːvən ˈspiːlbɜːrg/

14. Анджелина Джоли

15. −•−• •••• • •−•

16. Μπαράκ Ομπάμα

17. ⠧⠇⠁⠙⠊⠍⠊⠗ ⠏⠥⠞⠊⠝

18. مدونا

19. This Ancient Egyptian writing system had more than 1,000 distinct characters. What is it called?

20. This is Tifinagh, a script used to write the Tamazight family of languages spoken by more than 10 million people native to a cluster of half a dozen countries. Name any one of those countries.

ⵢⵍⵍⴰ ⵡⵉⵏ
ⵢⴻⵜⵜⵎⴻⵙⵍⴰⵢⴻⵏ
ⵜⴰⵏⴳⵍⵉⵣⵉⵜ ⴷⴰ?

21. This is how the name of the village of Kangiqsualujjuaq is written in the syllabic writing system of which language?

ᑲᖏᖅᓱᐊᓗᔾᔪᐊᖅ

22. What was the birth nationality of the person who wrote this?

$$i\hbar\frac{\partial}{\partial t}|\psi(t)\rangle = \hat{H}|\psi(t)\rangle$$

105 FROM HERE TO TIMBUKTU
Answers on page 211

How well do you know the African continent?

1. Timbuktu is frequently used as a metaphor for a distant place – but what country would you be in if you went there?

2. Which is Africa's busiest airport (by passenger numbers)?

3. Which country lies between Tanzania and Somalia?

4. Which one of these African countries was never a French colony? Algeria, Chad, Madagascar, Mozambique, Niger, Senegal.

5. Serengeti National Park is in which country?

6. Driving from Namibia to Kenya, what is the minimum number of countries you must pass through in between?

7. There are five living species of rhinoceros, and unfortunately three of them are under serious threat of extinction. How many of the five can be found in Africa?

8. Of the dozen or so subtropical deserts in the world, three are located in Africa. What are they called? (Hint: their names begin with S, K and N.)

9. In an alphabetical list of African countries, which would you find between Tunisia and Zambia?

10. Africa's highest mountain is in Tanzania. What is it called?

11. If you could walk 1,800km (1,100 miles) due south from the Algerian capital of Algiers without withering in the heat, which country would you end up in?

12. The Nile River is the longest river in the world. Which one of these countries does it not flow through? Egypt, Ethiopia, Kenya, Nigeria, Rwanda, Sudan, Uganda.

106 POINTS OF REFERENCE
Answers on page 212

All country borders have been removed from the European map below, leaving just the capital cities, some of which have been labelled. Can you match each of these listed capitals with the correct letter on the map?

1. Athens

2. Berlin

3. Copenhagen

4. Dublin

5. London

6. Luxembourg City

7. Madrid

8. Minsk

9. Paris

10. Prague

11. Pristina

12. Sarajevo

13. Vaduz

14. Vienna

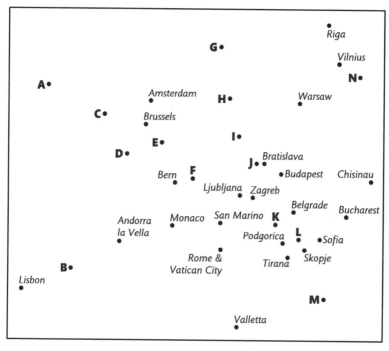

107 PAINT THE TOWN RED
Answers on page 212

Test your knowledge of celebrations around the world.

1. What is the name of the Bavarian beer festival that attracts more than 6 million tourists to Munich and the surrounding region each year?

2. The annual Songkran festival, often involving giant water fights in the street, marks New Year in which country?

3. The Japanese spring festival known as Hanami celebrates the appearance of what type of flowers?

4. Day of the Dead is a national holiday celebrated on the first two days of November in which country?

5. Every year, 40,000 or more people gather to indulge in a giant food fight in the streets of Buñol, eastern Spain, during which more than 100,000kg of what are thrown?

6. Moving to Italy but sticking with the theme of giant food fights, more than 250,000kg of what foodstuff is thrown in an epic three-day battle each February in Ivrea, near Turin?

7. What colour do people traditionally wear to celebrate the Dutch national holiday of Koningsdag (King's Day) every April?

8. Diwali – the festival of lights, symbolising victory of light over darkness, good over evil, and knowledge over ignorance – has its origins in the ancient harvest festivals of which country?

9. The Basque city of Pamplona is the setting for what famous event held each July?

10. While most of the world is celebrating New Year's Eve, which country celebrates Hogmanay?

11. The Hindu festival of spring – sometimes known as the festival of colours, as it is customary for people to throw vivid powder dyes on each other – goes by what four-letter name?

12. Harbin International Ice and Snow Sculpture Festival features some of the world's most impressive ice carvings. In which country is it held?

13. The Indianapolis 500 – often abbreviated to Indy 500 – is an annual car race held at the Indianapolis Motor Speedway in the US. To what does the '500' refer?

14. Saint Patrick's Day, the national day of Ireland, is celebrated around the world with parades, festivals, traditional Irish music and the wearing of green attire. In which month does it occur?

15. Which city's carnival, traditionally held over the two weeks running up to Lent, is famed for its ornate and elaborate masks?

16. The three largest LGBT Pride parades and festivals in the world are held in Madrid, New York, and which other city?

17. What is the name of the annual long-distance sled dog race run each March in Alaska, from Anchorage to Nome?

18. The End of Year (EOY) Cosplay Festival is a Japanese pop-cultural arts event held each year in which country?

19. The Burning Man festival is held every summer in the Black Rock Desert in which US state?

20. An unusual and frankly rather messy annual festival held every July since 1998 in Boryeong, South Korea, now attracts millions of visitors. What is the theme that this ten-day event is based around?

108 CITY SKYLINES
Answers on page 212

1. Built on reclaimed land and opened in 2012, this 101ha (250-acre) park is found in the centre of which city?

2. Which city is shown in this night-time cityscape?

3. This is the central district of which city, viewed from its harbour with the Royal Botanic Gardens in the foreground?

4. In which city would you find this scene?

5. The distinctive seafront area shown here is in the southern part of which major city?

6. This is the view from the top of the tallest structure in which city?

7. In which city would you find this 101-storey skyscraper, the world's tallest building until 2010 (but since surpassed by no fewer than nine others)?

8. Set against a mountainous backdrop, the skyline of which bustling seaport city is shown here?

109 BONES OF CONTENTION
Answers on page 212

1. Which territory is claimed by both Spain and the United Kingdom in a longstanding dispute over the wording of the 1713 Treaty of Utrecht?

2. Which province of Serbia unilaterally declared independence in 2008, being recognised by around 100 countries but not by Serbia?

3. Which peninsula, representing almost 5% of Ukraine's total area, was annexed by Russia following a military intervention in 2014? Six years on, some 18 countries now recognise the territory as Russian.

4. Which region is claimed by the partially recognised de facto sovereign state of the Sahrawi Arab Democratic Republic in a long-running battle for independence from Morocco?

5. France and Italy disagree over ownership of the peak of which mountain? France claims that the summit is entirely within its territory, while Italy maintains that the peak sits exactly on the shared border.

6. Which peninsula is claimed by two sovereign states that sit on either side of a heavily fortified 250km-long (160-mile) demilitarized zone, created in 1953 and known as the DMZ?

7. Which Indian Ocean island, that became an overseas department of France in 2011 (following a 95% referendum result), is the subject of a territorial dispute between France and the Comoros?

8. The rocky Senkaku Islands – formerly known as the Pinnacle Islands – are claimed by China and Taiwan, but are currently controlled by which country in dispute of these territorial claims? The disagreement is at risk of worsening as the territory includes valuable undersea oil reserves.

9. About which large region did a 1951 international treaty recognise that 'it is in the interest of all mankind that [it] shall continue forever to be used exclusively for peaceful purposes and shall not become the scene or object of international discord'? The agreement sets the area aside as a scientific preserve for all and bans military activity.

10. The ongoing dispute over control of which region was the principal cause of the four Indo-Pakistani wars, fought in 1947, 1965, 1971 and 1999?

110 EVERY DOG HAS HIS DAY
Answers on page 212

Match these dog breeds with their country of origin:

1.	Barak Hound	Australia
2.	Basenji	Bosnia & Herzegovina
3.	Chihuahua	Brazil
4.	Chinook	Canada
5.	Dalmatian	China
6.	Great Dane	Croatia
7.	Kangal Shepherd Dog	DR Congo
8.	Karelian Bear Dog	Finland
9.	Koolie	France
10.	Newfoundland	Germany
11.	Picardy Spaniel	Hungary
12.	Pug	Ireland
13.	Puli	Mexico
14.	Red Setter	Russia
15.	Samoyed	Tibet
16.	Serrano Bulldog	Turkey
17.	Shih Tzu	United Kingdom
18.	Whippet	USA

111 SCREEN TEST
Answers on page 212

For each film listed, enter into the corresponding line of the grid the name of the country where the majority of the action is set.

When completed, the shaded boxes will spell out vertically the title of another hit movie from 2008.

1. *Finding Nemo* (2003)

2. *The Beach* (2000)

3. *Doctor Zhivago* (1965)

4. *In Bruges* (2008)

5. *The Sweet Hereafter* (1997)

6. *Nacho Libre* (2006)

7. *Captain Corelli's Mandolin* (2001)

8. *The Reader* (2008)

9. *Evita* (1996)

10. *The Wind that Shakes the Barley* (2006)

11. *Blame It on the Bellboy* (1992)

12. *The Darjeeling Limited* (2007)

13. *The Wave* (2015)

14. *Lost in Translation* (2003)

15. *The Sound of Music* (1965)

16. *Ferdinand* (2017)

17. *Amélie* (2001)

18. *The Mummy* (1999)

112 WHERE AM I?
Answers on page 212

Below are some excerpts from postcards sent by travellers to their loved ones back home. Can you figure out the country each person is visiting?

1. This is the first time I've ever been on an island-hopping adventure – and what an adventure it's been! From lazing on secluded sandy beaches to strolling through the olive groves and citrus orchards in the Tragea Valley, it has all been so relaxing. I've swum in a volcanic caldera below a magical whitewashed village with little blue-domed churches built on a steep hillside, and spent an afternoon in a café playing tavli (kind of like backgammon) with the locals. It's been a blast!

2. This is such a vast country that you can't possibly hope to see everything on one visit. That's why we chose to focus this wildlife trip on the tropical wetland in the west. We've seen macaws, caimans, capybaras, howler monkeys and a tapir (in the distance) – but the crowning glory was a *very* lucky jaguar sighting. We didn't manage to find a giant anteater, unfortunately, but I guess that gives us a reason to come back!

3. Spent a long day yesterday hiking in the gorgeous Blue and John Crow Mountains National Park, so today I took it easy on Negril Beach at the other end of the island. Just had dinner (the local goat curry – yum!) and now fixing plans for my tour of the Appleton Rum Estate tomorrow. I still need to figure out whether I have the courage to do the Rainforest Bobsled down Mystic Mountain on my last day! Decisions, decisions...

4. We saw all the key sights on a river cruise – a blur of temples and tombs – before reaching the capital, where we spent an amazing day yesterday losing ourselves in the museum of antiquities. It's a higgledy-piggledy place in a cute pink colonial building just off Tahrir Square, packed to the gunnels with artifacts. You could spend a month in there! We're rather sad the trip's nearly over, but there's still time for a bit of souvenir shopping at the famous bazaar and souk in the historic city centre.

5. Right now I'm in the middle of the country in a city called Hue, on the banks of the Perfume River. I'm sitting in a place next door to my hostel, where you can get delicious bánh xèo (crispy stuffed rice pancakes) and wash it down with a refreshing bottle of '333' (5% lager) all for less than 35,000 dong – which is basically nothing! I hooked up with some other backpackers and we're headed for the Marble Mountains tomorrow.

6. Not the cheapest trip we've ever done, but *so* worth it. We self-drove the full length of the country's ring road and are now back in the capital. We've seen an iceberg-filled glacier lagoon, a black-sand beach that seemed to be glittering with diamonds, dramatic geysers, and more waterfalls than you could shake a stick at – but if I had to pick a best day, I'd have to say the whale-watching! We're planning to spend our final day in style at the Blue Lagoon, soaking in a geothermal pool and indulging ourselves with a full-body treatment of volcanic mud.

7. Apart from taking the obligatory hot-air balloon trip over the bizarre landscape of 'fairy chimneys', I've mostly avoided the tourist trail and have been having a whale of a time. Everyone's so welcoming, offering little glasses of tea at every turn! And I swear I've never before eaten as well as I have here. The traditional breakfasts are to die for: a veritable buffet of olives, cheeses, bread, sujuk spiced sausage and sometimes a delicious dish called 'menemen', made with eggs, tomato and peppers.

8. We went to a hypnotic two-hour noh performance – a type of traditional drama by an all-male troupe wearing carved masks and extravagant costumes, accompanied by four musicians and a chorus. The movements were slow and the language poetic (but dialogue was minimal so it wasn't so hard to follow the story). All of this was interspersed with comical interludes. Apparently this 600-year-old art form is protected as a UNESCO 'Intangible Cultural Heritage'.

9. I took the *El Chepe* through the foothills of the Sierra Madre, into picturesque pine forests and past deep gorges with rumbling rivers. At the end of the line is the mighty Copper Canyon. You only get a true feel for the sheer vastness of that place when you take the cable car: with the view from up there, you get some idea of what it means to be four times the size of the Grand Canyon. Back down on the ground, I hiked the Valley of the Frogs and the Valley of the Mushrooms. Today is a day of much-needed (and well deserved!) R&R at the hot springs.

10. We're really glad we took the advice to rent a campervan. It truly is the best way to appreciate the diverse and spectacular scenery here, from lush rolling hills to rainforest and farmland to seafront. We especially loved the route from Bay of Islands via Cape Reinga to Waipoua Forest then onto the Coromandel Peninsula. But the one thing that will stay with us long after this trip will be the memory of the wonderfully welcoming and friendly locals we've met at every step!

113 STRAIGHT AND NARROW
Answers on page 212

Can you identify each of the following long and narrow countries from their outlines?

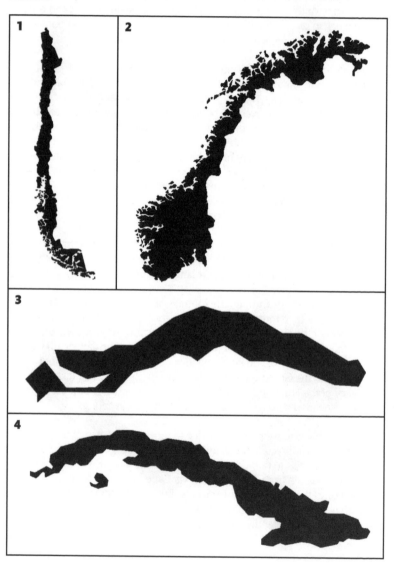

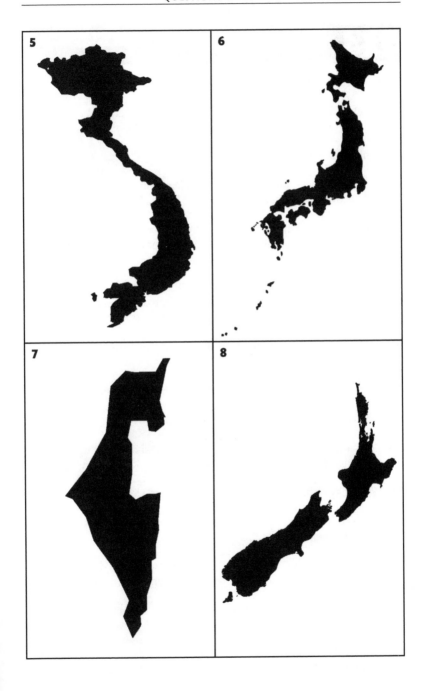

114 TINY TIM'S TREASURE TROVE

Answers on page 212

The answers to all of these general knowledge questions begin with 'T'.

1. What is the name of the bascule bridge over the River Thames that is raised around 800 times a year for the passing of tall ships?

2. What is Estonia's capital city called?

3. Meaning literally 'little cake', what is the name of the traditional Mexican flatbreads that date back around three millennia?

4. In which country did the death of a street vendor by self-immolation in 2010 catalyse the uprisings that came to be known at the Arab Spring?

5. What is the largest public square in Beijing?

6. Which ancient Egyptian pharaoh, whose tomb was discovered in 1922, restored the Ancient Egyptian religion after its dissolution by his father?

7. Which giant of Russian literature wrote *Anna Karenina*?

8. What fast upbeat folk dancing – typically in 6/8 time and accompanied by tambourines – is associated with southern Italy and Argentina?

9. Prenton Park in Birkenhead is the home ground of which football club?

10. What is the name for the nomadic pastoralists who inhabit the Sahara from Libya to Algeria, Niger, Mali, Burkina Faso and northern Nigeria?

11. Which city is the capital of Florida and home to Florida State University?

12. To which royal house did English monarchs Henry VIII, Edward VI and Elizabeth I belong?

13. Which brand of Swiss chocolate bar invented in 1908 is distinctively shaped and includes nougat, almonds and honey in the recipe?

14. Africa's largest lake is shared between four countries and drains into the Congo River system. What is it called?

15. Which British mathematician who played a crucial role in cracking Nazi codes in World War II is often called the Father of Modern Computing?

115 MEGACITIES
Answers on page 212

Use the Venn diagram below to categorise each of these big cities according to whether that city has ever hosted the Olympics (Summer or Winter), if it is in Asia, whether it is a capital city, and if it is a first city (that's to say, the most populous city of its country). No two cities belong in the same section.

1. Bangkok

2. Beijing

3. Cairo

4. Chicago

5. Mexico City

6. Mumbai

7. Nagano

8. Osaka

9. Rabat

10. São Paulo

11. Tokyo

12. Vancouver

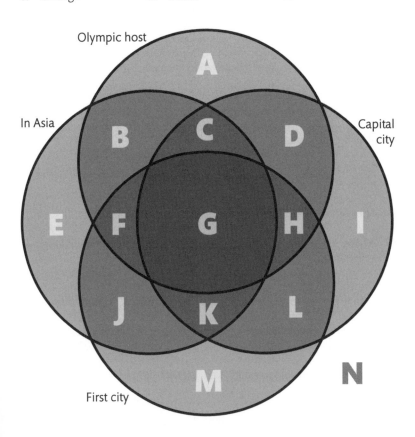

116 UNCLE SAM
Answers on page 212

Test your knowledge of the 50 states of the USA.

1. Which is the largest state after Alaska?

2. Two states have names beginning with K. What are they called?

3. Which state borders both California and Washington state?

4. In which state would you find the city of Baltimore?

5. The name of which state is an anagram of NOMINATES?

6. Which state is known as The Sunshine State?

7. In which state is the novel *To Kill a Mockingbird* set?

8. Which state has the largest population, with over 35% more people than the second most populous state?

9. In which state is the city of Phoenix?

10. Which three states have four-letter names?

11. The nickname 'Tar Heel' is used for which state, as well as for the sports teams and alumni of its largest university?

12. After Alaska, which state has the longest ocean coastline?

13. A famous symbol of American freedom, the Liberty Bell can be found in which state?

14. The 2005 film *Brokeback Mountain*, and the short story by Annie Proulx from which it was adapted, are set in the mountains of which state?

15. Each state has an official two-letter abbreviation. The abbreviations of which four states, written in sequence, spell out the word CONCORDE?

16. In which state would you find Pearl Harbor?

17. The four time zones of mainland USA are known by the acronyms EST, CST, MST and PST. What does 'EST' stand for?

18. And what does 'MST' stand for?

19. What is the state bird of Alabama?

20. The abbreviations for which four states spell out the word MANDARIN?

21. Which state is known as The Bluegrass State?

22. The easternmost point of the US mainland is in which state?

23. What city is the capital of the state of Texas?

24. In which state is the 1939 film *The Wizard of Oz* set?

25. How many states have names that begin with Y?

26. Rocky Mountain National Park is located in which state?

27. Arizona, California, Texas and which other state border Mexico?

28. The city of Anchorage is in which state?

29. The abbreviations for which four states spell out the word MEMORIAL?

30. The Mississippi River empties into which ocean basin?

31. Which of the states was the most recent to be admitted to the union?

32. People from which state are colloquially known as 'cheeseheads'?

33. The name of which state is an anagram of HAIRCUT SALOON?

34. Little Rock is the largest city in which state?

35. Which animal is featured on the state flag of California?

117 IN A SPIN
Answers on page 213

Enter the answers to the numbered clues into the spiral grid, from the outside inwards. Each answer shares its final letter with the first letter of the next answer. The boxes for the first and last letters of each answer (where the answers overlap) are shaded grey.

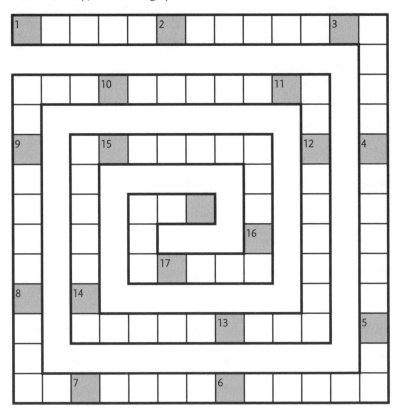

Once you have completed the spiral, rearrange the letters from the 18 shaded boxes to find the name of a nation with a large population of expats.

The number of letters in each answer is given in brackets after the clue.

1. A small country bordering Guatemala (6)

2. A mountain first successfully summited by Edmund Hillary and Tenzing Norgay, just hours before Queen Elizabeth II's coronation in 1953 (7)

3. An independent island nation in the South Pacific with nine islands and a population of just 12,000 (6)

4. The most populous post-Soviet state after Russia (7)

5. An African nation which follows a calendar that lags approximately seven years behind the Gregorian calendar used in most of the world (8)

6. The host city of the first modern Olympics, in 1896 (6)

7. The largest desert in the tropics (6)

8. The capital city of Turkey since the fall of the Ottoman Empire (6)

9. A central Italian town famed as the birthplace of St Francis, founder of the Franciscan religious order (6)

10. A republic in which the prime minister has been known by the title of Taoiseach – a local word meaning 'chief' – since 1937 (7)

11. The name of the official currency of Armenia (4)

12. The largest island in the Indian Ocean, located off Mozambique (10)

13. The most widely spoken Balto-Slavic language (7)

14. Kenya's capital city since 1907, located on a river of the same name (7)

15. The primary aboriginal language of the Canadian Arctic, belonging to the Eskimo–Aleut language family (9)

16. The largest living species of the big cats (5)

17. A style of popular music with its roots in Jamaica, developed from local variations on calypso and rhythm and blues, with influences from jazz, mento and traditional African folk (6)

118 A DROP IN THE OCEAN
Answers on page 213

Match each of these bodies of water with the corresponding locations marked
A–N on the map of Asia below.

1. Andaman Sea

2. Bay of Bengal

3. Celebes Sea

4. Coral Sea

5. Indian Ocean

6. Java Sea

7. Laccadive Sea

8. Pacific Ocean

9. Philippine Sea

10. Sea of Okhotsk

11. Solomon Sea

12. South China Sea

13. Timor Sea

14. Yellow Sea

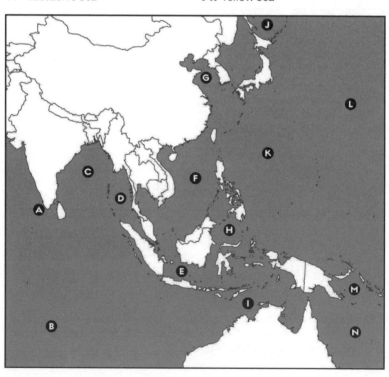

119 TOWER OF BABEL
Answers on page 213

The roots of the English language spread right around the globe. Match each trio of words below with the language from which they were adopted into English (in some cases via intermediary languages).

1.	alcohol, algebra, giraffe	Afrikaans
2.	alligator, hurricane, patio	Arabic
3.	apartheid, rooibos, trek	Cantonese
4.	avocado, chocolate, tomato	Czech
5.	bandana, guru, shampoo	Dutch
6.	beluga, gulag, vodka	French
7.	cartoon, graffiti, malaria	German
8.	cockatoo, orangutan, sarong	Hawaiian
9.	coffee, yoghurt, yurt	Hindi
10.	cookie, landscape, walrus	Italian
11.	country, journey, promenade	Japanese
12.	hula, ukulele, wiki	Malay
13.	karaoke, tsunami, tycoon	Nahuatl (Mexico)
14.	kowtow, lychee, wok	Russian
15.	pistol, polka, robot	Spanish
16.	poltergeist, rucksack, wanderlust	Turkish

120 FLIGHTS OF FANCY
Answers on page 213

Test your aviation knowledge with these questions on airports and airlines.

1. Which busy global hub airport, serving over 86 million passengers in 2019, has the official IATA code DXB?

2. What led to the cancellation or diversion of around a thousand flights at London's Gatwick Airport over a three-day period in late 2018?

3. What is the three-letter IATA code for Los Angeles International Airport?

4. Which airline has referred to itself as the 'Pride of Africa' since 2005?

5. In which country would you find Chhatrapati Shivaji Maharaj International Airport?

6. The airport on the island of Barra in Scotland, UK, handles around a thousand flights a year. What is unique about its runway?

7. In which country would you find Narita International Airport?

8. What do Mexico's Tijuana International Airport and Switzerland's Geneva Airport have in common with EuroAirport Basel Mulhouse Freiburg?

9. McCarran International Airport serves which US city?

10. Which airline changed its slogan from 'Hello Tomorrow' to 'Fly Better' in 2018?

11. Which airport is the world's busiest in terms of the number of passengers handled each year?

12. What unusual feature of their design do Hong Kong International Airport and Turkey's Ordu–Giresun Airport have in common with around half a dozen airports in Japan?

13. Which model of wide-body jet airliner is known as the 'Dreamliner'?

14. Which airline was founded in 1995 by Greek-Cypriot businessman Stelios Haji-Ioannou?

15. In which country did construction begin on Willy Brandt Airport in 2006, following 15 years of planning, with an intended opening date in 2011 – but a series of project overruns meant that this was delayed to 2012, 2013, 2017 and then 2020?

16. In 1996, in which city's international airport did Björk attack a journalist after stepping off a long flight?

17. On an aircraft, the announcement 'arm doors and cross-check' is an instruction from the flight deck for cabin crew to do what exactly?

18. Which city is served by the airport with the code BCN, formerly called El Prat Airport?

19. In which country do the vast majority of the three-letter IATA codes for airports begin with 'Y'? (This is because that country's codes derive from those historically used for weather reporting stations, and the 'Y' – short for 'yes' – indicated that the station was based at an airport.)

20. How many passenger terminals are there at London Heathrow Airport?

21. What unusual feature measuring 120m by 3,300m (400 by 11,000 ft) is located in the narrow strip between the two runways of Don Mueang International Airport in Thailand?

22. Which airline is the oldest in the world? It was founded over a century ago in 1919 and is still operating under its original name.

23. What do the IATA codes LON, PAR, NYC and MOW have in common?

24. At 5,402m (17,723 ft), the world's longest civilian runway is the record holder by a considerable margin: no other exceeds 5,000m (16,404 ft). In which country would you find it?

25. What unusual runway feature links Gibraltar International Airport with Gisborne Airport in New Zealand and Manakara Airport in Madagascar?

121 BRAND LOYALTY

Answers on page 213

Match each nation listed below with its world-famous brand.

1. Australia

2. Austria

3. Brazil

4. China

5. Czech Republic

6. Demark

7. Finland

8. France

9. Germany

10. Ireland

11. Italy

12. Japan

13. Netherlands

14. South Korea

15. Spain

16. Sweden

17. Switzerland

18. Taiwan

19. Turkey

20. United Kingdom

21. USA

A	B	C
ASUS®	beko	BURBERRY

D	E	F
EMBRAER	HARIBO	LEGO

122 MARK MY WORDS
Answers on page 213

Can you guess the missing words in the following quotations about travel?

1. *'Not all those who wander are ___.'*

– J R R Tolkien

2. *'Take only memories, leave only ___.'*

– Chief Seattle

3. *'A journey of a thousand miles begins with a ___ ___.'*

– Lao Tzu

4. *'The world is a book and those who do not travel read ___ ___ ___.'*
– widely attributed to Saint Augustine

5. *'Live with no excuses and travel with no ___.'*

– Oscar Wilde

6. *'I dislike feeling ___ ___ when I am abroad.'*

– George Bernard Shaw

7. *'A journey is best measured in ___ rather than miles.'*

– Tim Cahill

8. *'People don't take trips; ___ ___ ___.'*

– John Steinbeck

9. *'To unpathed waters, ___ shores, most certain.'*

– William Shakespeare

10. *'Life begins at the end of your ___ ___.'*

– Neale Donald Walsch

11. *'The real voyage of discovery consists not in seeking new landscapes, but in having new ___.'*

– Marcel Proust

12. *'I never travel without ___ ___. One should always have something sensational to read in the train.'*

– Oscar Wilde

13. 'Travel makes one modest; you see what a __ __ you occupy in the world.'
                                    – Gustave Flaubert

14. 'If you think adventure is dangerous, try __; it's lethal.'
                                    – Paul Coelho

15. '__ don't know where they've been, __ don't know where they're going.'
                                    – Paul Theroux

16. 'Like all great travellers, I have seen more than I remember and __ __ __
__ __ __.'
                                    – Benjamin Disraeli

17. 'Never go on trips with anyone you __ __ __.'
                                    – Ernest Hemingway

18. 'A journey is like marriage. The certain way to be wrong is to think you
__ it.'
                                    – John Steinbeck

19. 'To travel is to discover that __ __ __ about other countries.'
                                    – Aldous Huxley

20. 'Travelling tends to magnify all human __.'
                                    – Peter Hoeg

21. 'Life is short and the __ __ __, the sooner you start exploring it, the
better.'
                                    – Simon Raven

22. 'There are no __ __. It is the traveller only who is __.'
                                    – Robert Louis Stevenson

23. 'I haven't been everywhere, but it's __ __ __.'
                                    – Susan Sontag

24. 'When preparing to travel, lay out all your clothes and all your money.
Then take __ __ __ and __ __ __.'
                                    – Susan Heller

25. 'It is impossible to travel faster than the speed of light, and certainly not
desirable, as one's __ __ __ __.'
                                    – Woody Allen

123 AIN'T NO MOUNTAIN HIGH ENOUGH
Answers on page 213

1. Dubai's Burj Khalifa is the world's tallest building. How tall is Mount Everest by comparison? Roughly 10, 20, 30, 40, 50 or 60 times as tall?

2. Which is the highest mountain in the Alps?

3. The Mid-Atlantic Ridge is the world's longest mountain range, but which is the longest range that is *not* submerged?

4. Originally named Mount McKinley after the 25th US president, the USA's highest point was renamed to what by President Obama in 2015?

5. Which mountain range marks the division between Europe and Asia?

6. Which country's highest peak is called Aoraki or Mount Cook?

7. Mount Elbrus is located in which European mountain range?

8. Which country is entirely within the Pyrenees mountain range?

9. What is the world's second-highest mountain, after Mount Everest?

10. In which country would you find Mount Sinai?

11. Which geological time period is named after a mountain range that runs along the Swiss-French border between Geneva and Basel?

12. Toubkal is the highest peak in which North African mountain range?

13. In which country would you find the Mount of Olives (Mount Olivet)?

14. What is the name of the Alpine mountain known locally as Cervin?

15. The High Tatras are on the northern border of which European country?

16. Which of these is highest? La Paz (the world's highest capital), Mauna Kea, Mount Ararat, Mount Everest Base Camp, Mount Rainier.

17. In which country is the 5,426m (17,802 ft) Popocatépetl volcano?

18. Mount Shishaldin is said to be the world's most perfectly symmetrical conical mountain. In which country is it located?

124 WALK ON THE WILD SIDE
Answers on page 214

In the grid below, find the names of 20 animals you might spot while on safari in Africa. Words may run forwards or backwards in a vertical, horizontal or diagonal direction.

E	L	A	N	D	I	P	A	K	O
F	L	N	G	E	M	S	B	O	K
F	E	E	G	I	P	H	S	U	B
A	O	Y	P	Z	A	A	O	U	E
R	P	H	E	H	L	L	S	K	R
I	A	B	K	L	A	H	A	H	U
G	R	U	I	F	B	N	I	Y	T
A	D	R	F	A	S	N	T	R	L
U	O	U	B	N	O	I	L	A	U
G	B	Y	E	K	N	O	M	X	V

125 A PAIR OF CLUES
Answers on page 214

Each answer in this quiz is the answer to *two* of the questions. Match each question with its pair, and identify their shared answer.

1. A state on the east coast of the USA.

2. One of the five largest Tech Giants based in the US.

3. A DreamWorks animated movie franchise.

4. Crockery made of vitrified ceramic.

5. The movie in which Humphrey Bogart says 'here's looking at you, kid!'

6. A popular red wine grape variety also known as Syrah.

7. The mansion estate of Elvis Presley in Memphis, Tennessee.

8. London's largest railway station.

9. The US president who succeeded Ronald Reagan.

10. The most popular tourist destination among Muslim countries.

11. A citizen of one of Europe's most northern countries.

12. A blue cheese made in Derbyshire, Leicestershire or Nottinghamshire.

13. Nickname for a New Zealander.

14. The naturalist and geologist who lived at Down House in Kent.

15. Tiny particles ejected from a volcano.

16. A hard-shelled edible nut from the Amazon, with a triangular shape.

17. A type of boot worn and popularised by Duke Arthur Wellesley.

18. A dish of chicken in breadcrumbs, originating in the Russian Empire.

19. Africa's largest lake.

20. The capital city of Bulgaria.

21. A large Portuguese-speaking country.

22. A fruit also known as the Chinese gooseberry.

23. The primary port city of Morocco.

24. The most northerly of Australia's territory/state capitals.

25. A large Persian city sometimes known as the culture capital of Iran or the 'city of poets'.

26. The first name of the Colombian-born star of *Modern Family*.

27. The capital city of the Seychelles.

28. A huge rainforest straddling nine countries.

29. The European root vegetable known stateside as rutabaga.

30. A large bird of the genus *Meleagris*, native to the Americas.

31. Rural wilderness of Australia.

32. The seventh most populous capital city in Europe.

33. The fourth-largest island in the world, after Greenland, New Guinea and Borneo.

34. The most successful studio album of singer-songwriter Paul Simon.

35. The Belgian municipality famous as the site of Napoleon's final defeat.

36. The capital city of New Zealand.

37. The country with the world's largest number of military personnel.

38. A village in the county of Cambridgeshire, United Kingdom.

39. Trees of the genus *Fraxinus*, widespread in Europe and North America.

40. A post-Soviet country with a red-and-white flag.

126 TRIP OF A LIFETIME
Answers on page 214

It's some time since the five travellers in this puzzle made their special trips and they are all itching for another getaway!

Using the clues below, can you figure out where each went, in which year, and how long for? Complete the table using the logic grid to help you (by marking positive and negative relationships with ticks and crosses respectively). You will need to identify the destinations from their descriptions in the clues – for example if blue-footed boobies were mentioned, you would, of course, recognise the Galápagos. Each option in each category appears exactly once in the solution.

1. Coincidentally, no one visited a place beginning with the same letter as their name.

2. The ten-day holiday was not in the year directly before that of the person whose visit had been much enhanced by the country's locally produced Retsina and Ouzo!

3. Greg, whose holiday was two days longer than that of the person who had completed their experience by travelling to it on the luxurious *Blue Train*, was away either the year before or the year after the person whose holiday was two days shorter than Mel's.

4. The 16-day holiday in 2011 was to a place with the same initial as the person who had enjoyed a helicopter ride from Las Vegas, and whose holiday was four days shorter than Alex's which was in an earlier year than Lou's.

5. The person whose trip was two days longer than Val's didn't have the 2014 holiday.

		Destination					Year					Trip length				
		Acropolis (Athens)	Galápagos	Grand Canyon	Machu Picchu	Victoria Falls	2008	2009	2011	2013	2014	10 days	12 days	16 days	18 days	20 days
Name	Alex															
	Greg															
	Lou															
	Mel															
	Val															
Trip length	10 days															
	12 days															
	16 days															
	18 days															
	20 days															
Year	2008															
	2009															
	2011															
	2013															
	2014															

Name	Destination	Year	Trip length
Alex			
Greg			
Lou			
Mel			
Val			

127 RISE AND FALL OF THE ROMAN EMPIRE
Answers on page 214

With the help of the map below, how many of these cities can you identify from the names they had when they were part of the Roman Empire?

1. Andautonia

2. Aquae Sulis

3. Aquincum

4. Argentoratum

5. Londinium

6. Lugdunum

7. Lutetia

8. Mamucium

9. Massilia

10. Neapolis

11. Nida

12. Ragusium

13. Turicum

14. Venetiae

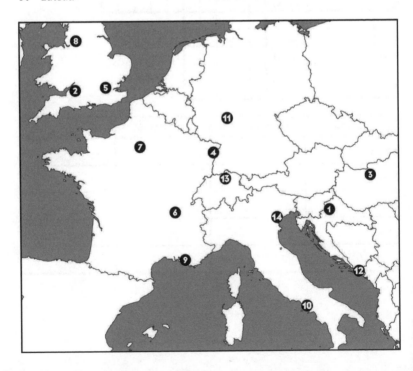

128 BREAK THE SPELL
Answers on page 214

This quiz is about countries that can be turned into other words or names with a small adjustment to their spelling.

1. Changing the middle letter of this country makes a sign of the zodiac.

2. Removing the final letter turns this country into a facial feature.

3. Changing the second letter to 'M' makes 2051 in Roman numerals.

4. Inserting a letter before the final one yields a triangular snack.

5. Adding a letter to the start makes a word for a lady.

6. Deleting its third letter turns it into the star of *Hannah Montana*.

7. Removing one of its vowels makes a recent British prime minister.

8. Swapping its two vowels turns it into a South American dance.

9. Changing the first letter makes a verb meaning to flounce or caper.

10. Adding a letter to the start creates a term for a type of diving.

11. Changing the first letter makes a Russian revolutionary and leader.

12. Swapping its two vowels turns it into an American rapper.

13. Changing its second vowel to a consonant makes the eggs of a frog.

14. Inserting a letter in the middle creates the most populous city in Nigeria.

15. Changing the first letter makes a vast region of Russia.

16. Removing the first letter turns it into the forename of the lead star in the 1978 film adaptation of a famous Broadway musical.

17. Changing the last letter creates the name of a neighbouring country.

18. Changing the first letter makes another country on the same continent.

129 IN ANOTHER WORLD
Answers on page 214

Most likely, you have travelled to several of the places mentioned in this book – and one day we hope you will get the chance to visit many of the others. But this quiz is about the some of the most extraordinary destinations to which only your imagination can transport you.

1. In which magical country, featured in a famous 1900 novel by L Frank Baum, does a road paved with yellow bricks lead to Emerald City?

2. Resting on the backs of four huge elephants, which are in turn carried upon the turtle Great A'Tuin, what flat realm is the fictional setting for more than 40 of Terry Pratchett's novels?

3. Which Irish satirist wrote the novel in which the protagonist visits Lilliput, Brobdingnag and Glubbdubdrib, among other places?

4. Reminiscent of medieval England, the fictional land of Westeros is the setting for which television fantasy drama series, based on a series of novels published from 1996?

5. Fred and Wilma Flintstone, and their next-door neighbours the Rubbles, live in what Stone Age town?

6. Mr Tumnus, Reepicheep the Mouse and Jadis the White Witch are inhabitants of which other world, which was named after a small town in central Italy by author C S Lewis?

7. What is the name of the world where the Warcraft series of video games – along with the numerous spin-off novels and comics – are set?

8. The events described in J R Tolkien's best-known works, *The Hobbit* and *The Lord of the Rings*, take place on which fictional landmass?

9. In which real-world country would you find Moomin World, a theme park celebrating the lives of Moominpappa, Moominmamma, Moomintroll and their friends from Moominvalley? (It is the homeland of the author and illustrator of the original books, published between 1945 and 1993.)

10. In the universe of Harry Potter, the Beauxbatons Academy of Magic is located in which real-world country?

11. Who wrote the novel in which a young girl falls through a rabbit hole into a subterranean fantasy world populated by extraordinary creatures, including the March Hare, the Cheshire Cat and the Mock Turtle?

12. What is the name of the town where animated television characters Lisa, Maggie and Bart live with their parents Homer and Marge?

13. First published in 1974 and adapted for television some years later, Tom Sharpe's satirical look at university life is set in which fictional Cambridge college?

14. Which series of action role-playing video games takes place on the imaginary continent of Tamriel?

15. In the children's stories by A A Milne, what is the name for the area of forest where Winnie-the-Pooh, Tigger, Eeyore, Piglet and Rabbit live?

16. Which mighty world from Norse mythology provides the setting for the 2011 movie *Thor* and its sequels?

17. Intelligent dinosaurs and shipwrecked humans live and work together harmoniously in a series of more than 20 books created by author and illustrator James Gurney and his collaborators. What is the name of the isolated island that provides the setting for these stories, as well as their subsequent television, film and video game adaptations?

18. Which radio drama is based around life in the fictional village of Ambridge in the equally fictional English county of Borsetshire? It is the world's longest-running drama, having begun in 1950.

19. On which mythical island does Peter Pan spend his endless childhood with Tinker Bell, Captain Hook, the Lost Boys and an assortment of beasts?

20. Which popular children's television series presents railway-based adventures set on the fictional British island of Sodor?

130 BITTEN BY THE TRAVEL BUG
Answers on page 214

Across

1. Scottish delicacy banned in the US (6)

4. Purpose of winter trip to mountains (6)

9 and 31 across. Traditional anti-malarial (5,5)

10. Japanese paper art (7)

11 and 12 across. Euphoria, as when travelling for instance (5,7)

12. *See 11 across*

13. Food not on pollo-pescetarian menu (3,4)

15. Ursine icon of China (5)

17. European root vegetable, also called pignut (5)

18. Naval flags (7)

20. Progress on tough journey (4,7)

24. Restaurant food to go (7)

25. Subarctic coniferous region (5)

26. *See 7 down*

28. Provoked by continual questioning (7)

29. Large marine crustacean (7)

31. *See 9 across*

33. Descriptive of scientific garden found in many major cities (7)

34. Southwest Pacific island nation (5)

35. Dutch city famous for WWII battle (6)

36 across and 5 down. Versatile tool when camping (6,5)

Down

1. Set out on a journey (3,3,4)

2. Edible fruit from the New World, also known as Spanish lime (5)

3. Impulse to travel (5,4)

5. *See 36 across*

6. Persian (7)

7 down and 26 across. Splitting the bill (5,5)

8. Travel to unusual destinations (2,3,3,6,5)

14. Country where Lego comes from (7)

15. Assumed instagrammable stance with selfie stick (5)

16. Church recess (4)

Questions continued overleaf

19. Fish-eating crocodile from Indian subcontinent (7)

21. Geological time period (5)

22. Traction device on snow tyres (4)

23. Irresistible desire to roam (10)

25. Korean martial art (3,4,2)

27. Language spoken in world's highest region (7)

29. Saharan nation (5)

30. Kazakhstani currency (5)

32. Large suitcase or travel chest (5)

ANSWERS

1. **East is East: 1.** Genghis Khan (born Temüjin Borjigin); **2.** lion; **3.** Japan; **4.** 17th century (1632–53); **5.** Seoul; **6.** Borneo; **7.** Sri Lanka; **8.** a lake; **9.** yakitori (Japanese skewered chicken); **10.** four; **11.** Saigon River; **12.** Hinduism; **13.** Dhaka; **14.** Korean; **15.** tai chi (Chinese).

2. **Food for thought: 1.** Mexico; **2.** Greece; **3.** Japan; **4.** Sweden; **5.** Brazil; **6.** China; **7.** South Africa; **8.** Thailand; **9.** USA; **10.** Belgium; **11.** Italy; **12.** South Korea; **13.** Hungary; **14.** United Kingdom; **15.** Switzerland; **16.** Colombia; **17.** Jamaica; **18.** Ethiopia; **19.** Spain; **20.** Iran.

3. **Rebranding: 1.** Sri Lanka; **2.** Istanbul; **3.** Myanmar; **4.** Saigon; **5.** Eswatini (written 'eSwatini' in the local language); **6.** Bombay; **7.** Upper Volta; **8.** Saint Petersburg; **9.** Zaire; **10.** Nur-Sultan; **11.** Cecil Rhodes (the country was Southern Rhodesia and later Rhodesia); **12.** New Amsterdam; **13.** Cambodia; **14.** Victoria, Australia; **15.** Japan (capital city: Tokyo); **16.** Thailand; **17.** Madras; **18.** Salisbury; **19.** Tasmania; **20.** Beijing.

4. **Streets ahead: 1.** Arc de Triomphe (in Place Charles de Gaulle); **2.** Wall Street; **3.** La Rambla or Las Ramblas; **4.** Khao San Road; **5.** Via Dolorosa (Way of Suffering); **6.** Downing Street; **7.** Royal Mile; **8.** Istanbul; **9.** Stradun; **10.** San Francisco; **11.** Australia (in Gold Coast, Adelaide, Wedderburn, and the last two in Melbourne); **12.** Singapore.

5. **Chart topper: 1.** B; **2.** F; **3.** E; **4.** A; **5.** C; **6.** D.

6. **Landmarks of the New World: 1.** G/Moai statues (Easter Island); **2.** C/Statue of Liberty (New York City, USA); **3.** B/CN Tower (Toronto, Canada); **4.** D/Vincent Thomas Bridge (Los Angeles, USA); **5.** E/Teotihuacan (Mexico); **6.** A/Space Needle (Seattle, USA); **7.** H/Christ the Redeemer (Rio de Janeiro, Brazil); **8.** F/Bridge of the West (Colombia).

7. **The Seven Seas (and a dozen more):** Aegean (Sea), Andaman (Sea), Arabian (sea), Aral (Sea), Arctic (Ocean), Argentine (Sea), Barents (Sea), Bering (Sea), Black (Sea), Ionian (Sea), Irish (Sea), (Sea of) Japan, Java (Sea), Labrador (Sea), Libyan (Sea), Molucca (Sea), Solomon (Sea), South China (Sea), Tasman (Sea).

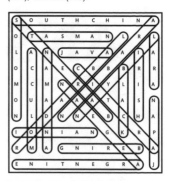

8. **Peter Piper's pickled peppers: 1.** Piccadilly Circus; **2.** Parthenon; **3.** Pristina (or Prishtina); **4.** Portugal; **5.** pangolins; **6.** Persian Gulf; **7.** Petronas Towers; **8.** Prague; **9.** Pyongyang; **10.** Paraguay; **11.** Peloponnese; **12.** Palermo; **13.** panda; **14.** Phnom Penh (Cambodia); **15.** Puerto Rico.

9. **Bradt Travel Guides: 1.** Bulgari (stylised as BVLGARI); **2.** *Ratatouille*; **3.** Agadir; **4.** Dalai Lama; **5.** tae kwon do; **6.** Trinidad and

Tobago; **7.** raccoon; **8.** Auschwitz (formerly Auschwitz concentration camp, now Auschwitz-Birkenau State Museum); **9.** Vatican City; **10.** Elizabeth Tower; **11.** Luxor; **12.** Gaddafi; **13.** Urdu; **14.** Imran; **15.** Denmark; **16.** ethnic cleansing; **17.** sake.

10. **Picture postcard: 1.** Terracotta Army (Shaanxi, China); **2.** Brussels (Manneken Pis); **3.** Argentina; **4.** Philippines; **5.** Machu Picchu; **6.** Budapest (Fisherman's Bastion); **7.** Fish River Canyon; **8.** Bridge of Sighs in Venice, Italy.

11. **A rising star: 1.** Australia/6 stars; **2.** Bangladesh/no stars; **3.** Brazil/ 27 stars; **4.** Cape Verde/10 stars; **5.** China/5 stars; **6.** Cook Islands/15 stars; **7.** European Union/12 stars; **8.** Grenada/7 stars; **9.** New Zealand/ 4 stars; **10.** Philippines/3 stars (not counting the Sun); **11.** Syria/2 stars; **12.** Turkey/1 star; **13.** Tuvalu/9 stars; **14.** USA/50 stars; **15.** Venezuela/8 stars.

12. **Followed to the letter: 1.** San Marino; **2.** Chad, Cuba, Fiji, Iran, Iraq, Laos, Mali, Niue, Oman, Peru, Togo; **3.** Peru; **4.** Colombia; **5.** Switzerland; **6.** Seychelles; **7.** United Arab Emirates, with 18 letters (other good answers: Dominica, Kiribati and Suriname, with 8 letters each); **8.** Vilnius; **9.** Mozambique; **10.** Greece; **11.** Micronesia; **12.** The only vowel in all these names is A, except for Morocco (whose only vowel is O); **13.** Belgrade (Serbia), Bern (Switzerland), Bratislava (Slovakia), Bucharest (Romania) and Budapest (Hungary); **14.** Peru; **15.** Sweden is an anagram of WEDNES(day).

13. **Night at the museum: 1.** England, United Kingdom; **2.** Iceland; **3.** Paris, France; **4.** India; **5.** USA; **6.** Baku, Azerbaijan; **7.** Oslo, Norway; **8.** London (the British Museum, Tate Modern, National Gallery and Natural History Museum were the 5th, 6th, 7th and 8th most-visited museums globally in 2019); **9.** Croatia; **10.** Croatia, again!; **11.** Louvre, Paris; **12.** Japan; **13.** Ashmolean Museum; **14.** Mexico; **15.** National Air and Space Museum; **16.** Victoria and Albert Museum (V&A); **17.** Barcelona; **18.** Brussels, Belgium; **19.** Dublin, Ireland (Guinness Storehouse); **20.** Metropolitan Museum of Art ('the Met').

14. **Jules Verne adventure:** *Across:* **7.** Bern; **8.** cable car; **9.** Dartmoor; **10.** sake; **11.** skol; **14.** Hawaiian; **16.** tusk; **18.** Fogg; **20.** indirect; **23.** aglu. *Down:* **1.** Newark; **2.** Anatolia; **3.** ICAO; **4.** Aberdeen; **5.** Ness; **6.** Baikal; **12.** twilight; **13.** outbreak; **15D/12A/21A/21D.** Around the World in Eighty Days; **17.** Sicily; **19.** grid.

15. **Fountains of fire: 1.** Mount Vesuvius; **2.** Ring/Rim of Fire; **3.** Giant's Causeway; **4.** Iceland; **5.** Mauna Kea; **6.** The Andes; **7.** White Island or Whakaari; **8.** Sicily; **9.** aa or a'a; **10.** Krakatoa; **11.** lava tube; **12.** British Airways.

16. **Water, water everywhere: 1.** D; **2.** B; **3.** A; **4.** J; **5.** M; **6.** N; **7.** E; **8.** G; **9.** F; **10.** I; **11.** L; **12.** K; **13.** H; **14.** C.

17. **Life down under: 1.** Coral Sea; **2.** Auckland; **3.** didgeridoo (also known as a dronepipe); **4.** haka (the specific one usually performed is called Ka Mate but on some special occasions since 2005 they have

used a haka called Kapa O Pango);
5. eucalyptus leaves; **6.** *Where the Wild Things Are* (filmed in Australia); **7.** Great Ocean Road; **8.** 12; **9.** Canberra; **10.** Christchurch; **11.** a liquor store; **12.** Netherlands; **13.** opal; **14.** it is their name for New Zealand; **15.** possum; **16.** Tasman Sea; **17.** Giant Caterpillar; **18.** a wing of the parliament (containing the prime minister's office); **19.** New Zealand; **20.** Waikato; **21.** penicillin (shared with Alexander Fleming and Ernst Boris Chain); **22.** Jenny Shipley (in 1997); **23.** Great Victoria Desert; **24.** Waitangi; **25.** it's a famous example among linguists – the Mbabaram word for dog was coincidentally also 'dog' well before the first English speakers arrived in Australia.

18.   Unconventional safaris: Angela/ Botswana/Penny-farthing/Lion; Bertie/Kenya/Donkey riding/Rhino; Carmen/Tanzania/Pogo stick/ Buffalo; Darcelle/Gabon/Sedan chair/ Elephant; Emil/Zambia/Hovercraft/ Leopard.

19.   She sells sea shells: 1. Scandinavia; **2.** Seychelles; **3.** Slovenia; **4.** Sydney Harbour Bridge; **5.** Sofia; **6.** Seine; **7.** Santa Fe; **8.** Santorini; **9.** Stuttgart; **10.** Saskatchewan; **11.** Skytree; **12.** Sweden; **13.** Sarajevo; **14.** Sudan; **15.** Seoul (South Korea).

20.   Making a name for yourself:
1. Albania/Shqipëria; **2.** Belgium/ Belgique; **3.** Croatia/Hrvatska; **4.** Egypt/Misr; **5.** Finland/Suomi; **6.** Germany/Deutschland; **7.** Greece/ Hellas; **8.** Greenland/Kalaallit Nunaat; **9.** Hungary/Magyarország; **10.** Ireland/Éire; **11.** Japan/Nippon; **12.** Norway/Norge.

21.   Treasure island: 1. Sri Lanka; **2.** Tasmania (Australia); **3.** Isabela (the largest of the Galápagos Islands, Ecuador); **4.** Madagascar; **5.** Spitsbergen (the largest island in Svalbard, Norway); **6.** Cyprus; **7.** Iceland; **8.** Easter Island (Chile); **9.** Hispaniola (comprising Haiti and the Dominican Republic); **10.** Guadeloupe (an overseas region of France) – technically this is *two* islands, but the gap between them is just 60m wide and spanned by two bridges; **11.** Borneo (comprising Brunei along with parts of Malaysia and Indonesia); **12.** Sicily (Italy).

22.   City lights: 1. Poland; **2.** Egypt; **3.** Germany; **4.** Brazil; **5.** Netherlands; **6.** Morocco; **7.** France; **8.** Croatia; **9.** South Africa; **10.** Peru; **11.** Portugal; **12.** India; **13.** Switzerland; **14.** Israel; **15.** Belarus; **16.** Turkey; **17.** Syria; **18.** Cuba. *City nickname:* Pearl of the Adriatic (Dubrovnik).

23.   Tunnel vision: 1. Budapest, Hungary; **2.** Los Angeles, USA; **3.** Stockholm, Sweden; **4.** Athens, Greece; **5.** Pyongyang, North Korea.

24.   At a loss for words: 1. French; **2.** Italian; **3.** Wales; **4.** German; **5.** Portuguese; **6.** fromage; **7.** Malta; **8.** looking for three paws on a cat; **9.** potatoes; **10.** Turkish; **11.** house; **12.** Finland.

25.   The call of the wild: 1. South Africa; **2.** Yosemite; **3.** Seychelles (the Aldabra giant tortoise lives on Aldabra atoll); **4.** Indonesia; **5.** Galápagos penguin (Humboldt penguins can also be found quite close to the equator but the northernmost extent of their range stops about 600km/370 miles short); **6.** monkeys; **7.** Cairngorms; **8.** Costa Rica; **9.** Greenland

(Northeast Greenland National Park); **10.** 400 thousand (IUCN estimate in 2016); **11.** Madagascar; **12.** Chile; **13.** two; **14.** Zambia; **15.** Borneo; **16.** Yellowstone; **17.** great white pelican; **18.** China; **19.** Serengeti National Park in Tanzania; **20.** northeast; **21.** South America; **22.** Canada; **23.** Croatia; **24.** spectacled bear, also known as Andean bear or mountain bear; **25.** New Zealand.

26. **You get the next round: 1.** A; **2.** K; **3.** H; **4.** T; **5.** L; **6.** G; **7.** D; **8.** P; **9.** N; **10.** I; **11.** E; **12.** Q; **13.** J; **14.** C; **15.** F; **16.** U; **17.** S; **18.** B; **19.** O; **20.** R; **21.** M.

27. **Dr Livingstone, I presume? 1.** L; **2.** D; **3.** A; **4.** F; **5.** C; **6.** I; **7.** B; **8.** K; **9.** J; **10.** E; **11.** H; **12.** G.

28. **Chain reaction: 1.** Portugal (Vasco da Gama Bridge in Lisbon); **2.** Spain; **3.** France; **4.** Switzerland (CERN's Large Hadron Collider); **5.** Austria; **6.** Hungary; **7.** Romania; **8.** Bulgaria; **9.** Turkey; **10.** Iran; **11.** Pakistan; **12.** India (Indian Rupee); **13.** Myanmar; **14.** Laos; **15.** Cambodia.

29. **Words of wisdom: 1.** Gettysburg, Pennsylvania (Gettysburg Address by Abraham Lincoln in 1863); **2.** Indian (Mahatma Gandhi, speaking in 1931); **3.** France (René Descartes in *Discourse on the Method*, 1637); **4.** Stephen Hawking; **5.** Ich bin ein Berliner; **6.** Winston Churchill; **7.** Malala Yousafzai; **8.** Washington DC (from the steps of the Lincoln Memorial); **9.** Douglas Adams (in *Mostly Harmless*); **10.** Neil Armstrong; **11.** Karl Marx; **12.** Amsterdam (Anne Frank in her first diary entry); **13.** Albert Einstein (explaining

relativity); **14.** Nelson Mandela; **15.** Greta Thunberg.

30. **Round the twist: 1.** Newcastle; **2.** earthquake; **3.** Egyptologist; **4.** Transylvania; **5.** Australia; **6.** alligator; **7.** ravioli; **8.** Islamabad; **9.** Dijon; **10.** Nutcracker; **11.** Rotterdam; **12.** Mayotte. *Anagram: Mediterranean.*

31. **A rose by any other name: 1.** Ireland; **2.** New Orleans, Louisiana; **3.** Iceland; **4.** Rome, Italy; **5.** Ukraine; **6.** Birmingham, UK; **7.** South Africa; **8.** Dundee, Scotland, UK; **9.** Chile; **10.** Chicago, Illinois; **11.** Finland; **12.** Macau; **13.** France; **14.** New York City; **15.** New Zealand; **16.** Dublin; **17.** Madagascar; **18.** Singapore; **19.** Canada; **20.** Tasmania, Australia.

32. **By popular demand: 1.** D; **2.** G; **3.** J; **4.** C; **5.** A; **6.** I; **7.** B; **8.** H; **9.** E; **10.** F.

33. **Thirty-three three-word answers: 1.** Alexander Nevsky Cathedral; **2.** Asahi Super Dry; **3.** Bay of Biscay; **4.** Bridge of Sighs; **5.** Cannes Film Festival; **6.** Dar es Salaam; **7.** Edinburgh Fringe Festival; **8.** Etosha National Park; **9.** Great Barrier Reef; **10.** Golden Gate Bridge; **11.** *Gorilla gorilla gorilla*; **12.** Hammersmith and City; **13.** Hay-on-Wye; **14.** Isles of Scilly; **15.** James Bond Island; **16.** Just for Laughs; **17.** Los Angeles Philharmonic; **18.** Las Vegas Raiders; **19.** Lotte World Tower; **20.** Port-au-Prince; **21.** Prince Edward Island; **22.** Royal Air Maroc; **23.** Red Bull Ring; **24.** Royal Caribbean International; **25.** Rio de Janeiro; **26.** Sydney Opera House; **27.** Statue of Liberty; **28.** Tristan da Cunha; **29.** Trans-Mongolian Railway; **30.** Universal Studios Florida; **31.** Van Gogh Museum; **32.** Wolfgang

Amadeus Mozart; **33.** Way Out West.

34. Double Dutch: 1. French ('flammable material: no smoking'), **2.** Tagalog/Filipino ('no littering'), **3.** Italian ('warning! risk of falling in sea: keep away'), **4.** Spanish ('caution! slippery when wet'), **5.** Finnish ('beware of weak ice and channels'), **6.** Afrikaans ('beware of hippos'), **7.** Polish ('caution! frogs on road'), **8.** Turkish ('beware of the dog'), **9.** German ('keep off the grass'), **10.** Vietnamese ('warning! do not pass'), **11.** Portuguese ('attention! no parking: loading and unloading day and night'), **12.** Icelandic ('warning! area closed to all traffic due to dangerous geysers'), **13.** Hungarian ('attention! area protected by cameras and dogs'), **14.** Welsh ('in the interest of public health do not feed the seagulls'), **15.** Czech ('caution! border zone: entry with permit only'), **16.** Tok Pisin/New Guinea Pidgin ('turn on your headlights').

35. The Spanish Inquisition: 1. Granada; **2.** Pablo Picasso; **3.** Barcelona; **4.** Castelo Branco (it's in Portugal); **5.** Bilbao; **6.** Balearic Islands; **7.** wild/rugged coast; **8.** Iberia; **9.** São Miguel (it's a Portuguese island in the Azores); **10.** three (Portugal, France and Andorra); **11.** peseta; **12.** Sierra Nevada; **13.** AVE (Alta Velocidad Española); **14.** ballpoint pen; **15.** Menorca.

36. Pigs might fly: 1. D (also known as the African penguin); **2.** J; **3.** G; **4.** F; **5.** I; **6.** A; **7.** C; **8.** B; **9.** H; **10.** L; **11.** K; **12.** E.

37. Staying on track: 1. bullet trains; **2.** New Street (it is Birmingham's main train station); **3.** Tokyo, Japan; **4.** *Orient Express*; **5.** Grand Central Station/Terminal, New York; **6.** Moscow; **7.** Sri Lanka; **8.** China (at Tanggula Pass on the Qinghai–Tibet railway); **9.** France (Train à Grande Vitesse); **10.** Pullman cars/coaches; **11.** Iran (in fact, its rail network is amongst the 20 most extensive in the world); **12.** South Africa (between Pretoria and Cape Town); **13.** *Eurostar* (cars and cargo are carried on the same line by *Eurotunnel Shuttle*); **14.** Penzance (the other two connect London with Scotland); **15.** Bangkok, Thailand; **16.** Argentina; **17.** Mumbai, India; **18.** Sweden and Denmark; **19.** Russia (between Moscow and Saint Petersburg); **20.** Australia; **21.** Turkey (Istanbul); **22.** *Mallard*; **23.** Canada; **24.** Singapore (although some existed prior to 1927); **25.** *Maharajas' Express*.

38. Get your money's worth: *Across:* **8.** Egypt; **9.** Orinoco; **10.** foreign; **11.** rupee; **12.** Joseph; **13.** Istria; **15.** prepay; **17.** Turkey; **20.** nacre; **22.** afghani; **24.** sporran; **25.** evade. *Down:* **1.** pelf; **2.** Cyprus; **3.** Ethiopia; **4.** pound; **5.** birr; **6.** copper; **7.** monetary; **12.** Japanese; **14.** smuggler; **16.** escrow; **18.** koalas; **19.** pawns; **21.** euro; **23.** item.

39. Chalk and cheese: 1. Coalho/Brazil; **2.** Feta/Greece; **3.** Gorgonzola/Italy; **4.** Gouda/Netherlands; **5.** Gruyère/Switzerland; **6.** Halloumi/Cyprus; **7.** Lighvan/Iran; **8.** Limburger/Belgium; **9.** Manchego/Spain; **10.** Monterey Jack/USA; **11.** Oaxaca/Mexico; **12.** Oscypek/Poland; **13.** Roquefort/France; **14.** Tulum/Turkey; **15.** Wensleydale/United Kingdom.

40. World literature: 1. Norwegian; **2.** Portuguese; **3.** Victor Hugo; **4.** Russian; **5.** *The Girl with the Dragon Tattoo*; **6.** Japanese; **7.** French;

8. Miguel de Cervantes; **9.** Swedish;
10. The Little Prince; **11.** Umberto
Eco; **12.** Czech (Milan Kundera
became a French citizen in 1981).

41. **Landmarks of Western Europe:**
    1. J/Tower of Pisa (Italy); **2.** G/
    Atomium (Brussels, Belgium); **3.** F/
    Louvre Museum (Paris, France); **4.** B/
    Belem Tower (Lisbon, Portugal); **5.** A/
    Hallgrímskirkja (Reykjavik, Iceland);
    6. E/Tower Bridge (London, UK); **7.** D/
    Sagrada Familia (Barcelona, Spain);
    8. K/Colosseum (Rome, Italy); **9.** H/
    Ejer Bavnehøj (Denmark); **10.** C/
    Segovia Aqueduct (Spain); **11.** L/White
    Tower (Thessaloniki, Greece); **12.** I/
    Brandenburg Gate (Berlin, Germany).

42. **All shook up: 1.** Grenada;
    2. Russian; **3.** Menorca; **4.** Montana;
    5. Sistine Chapel; **6.** Amsterdam;
    7. Tasmania (where the Tasmanian
    devil lives); **8.** Siberian; **9.** Islamabad;
    10. Stromboli; **11.** Nassau;
    12. Southern Rhodesia (now called
    Zimbabwe); **13.** Vietnamese;
    14. Belgrade; **15.** Copenhagen; **16.** Las
    Vegas; **17.** Trinidad; **18.** Nova Scotia;
    19. Taiwan; **20.** Switzerland; **21.** Statue
    of Liberty; **22.** The Hilton; **23.** Angela
    Merkel; **24.** Algeria; **25.** Manila; **26.** El
    Salvador; **27.** The Leaning Tower of
    Pisa; **28.** Milton Keynes; **29.** Palestine;
    30. Wolfgang Amadeus Mozart.

43. **A River Runs Through It:** Amazon,
    Clyde, Congo, Danube, Euphrates,
    Ganges, Hudson, Indus, Irrawaddy,
    Loire, Niger, Nile, Orinoco, Rhine,
    Rhone, Seine, Thames, Volga, Yangtze,
    Yarra, Zambezi.

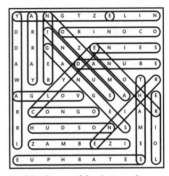

44. **Beside the seaside: 1.** Australia;
    2. two; **3.** Rio de Janeiro, Brazil;
    4. Greece; **5.** vodka; **6.** lifeguard on
    duty; **7.** Jurassic Coast; **8.** Danny
    Boyle; **9.** Hawaii; **10.** pelajar
    (it means 'student' in Malay);
    11. Portugal; **12.** Cape Town, South
    Africa; **13.** Vietnam; **14.** *Cast Away*;
    15. flotsam is lost by accident in
    a shipwreck whereas jetsam is
    deliberately thrown overboard by a
    ship's crew to lighten the load in an
    emergency.

45. **Letter to the Editor:** Anna/Zanzibar/
    9th/Thursday; Carys/Guyana/3rd/
    Monday; Heather/Socotra/1st/
    Tuesday; Laura/Madagascar/13th/
    Wednesday; Susannah/Oman/4th/
    Friday.

46. **No man is an island: 1.** France;
    2. Falkland Islands; **3.** Balearic
    Islands (Islas Baleares); **4.** Cuba;
    5. Honshu; **6.** Malta; **7.** Rapa Nui;
    8. Sicily; **9.** Jamaica; **10.** Hawaii;
    11. Alcatraz; **12.** New Zealand;
    13. Borneo; **14.** Tristan da Cunha;
    15. Canary Islands (Islas Canarias);
    16. British (written by H G Wells
    and William Golding respectively);
    17. Japan; **18.** Nova Scotia;
    19. Mont-Saint-Michel; **20.** Zanzibar;
    21. Brazil (offshore from São Paulo);
    22. Galveston Island (it's just south of

Houston in Texas); **23.** *Island of Lost Souls*; **24.** Bahamas; **25.** Sandwich Islands.

47.   Safety in numbers: 1. two (blue and yellow); **2.** 12; **3.** three (United Kingdom, France and Spain); **4.** one (the whole country follows Beijing Time); **5.** seven; **6.** eight; **7.** 96; **8.** six; **9.** three (Belize, Guatemala, USA); **10.** two (Spain and Portugal); **11.** three (African bush elephant, African forest elephant and Asian elephant); **12.** three (Ohio, Oklahoma, Oregon); **13.** three (Pakistan–Iran–Turkey–Greece); **14.** eight (the clock has four faces, each with two hands); **15.** two (in 1978 and 1986).

48.   Everybody needs good neighbours: Madagascar (0 neighbours), Portugal (1 neighbour), USA (2 neighbours), Finland (3 neighbours), Thailand (4 neighbours), Peru (5 neighbours), Iraq (6 neighbours), Sudan (7 neighbours), Tanzania (8 neighbours), Germany (9 neighbours), Brazil (10 neighbours).

49.   In vino veritas: 1. K; **2.** P; **3.** E; **4.** D; **5.** F; **6.** O; **7.** L; **8.** Q; **9.** J; **10.** N; **11.** M; **12.** I; **13.** T; **14.** A; **15.** H; **16.** G; **17.** R; **18.** S; **19.** B; **20.** C.

50.   Wonders of the World: 1. Prague; **2.** Rome; **3.** New York; **4.** Madrid; **5.** Amsterdam; **6.** Paris; **7.** Tokyo; **8.** Jaipur; **9.** Istanbul; **10.** Moscow; **11.** Venice; **12.** Dubai; **13.** Barcelona; **14.** Cardiff; **15.** Beijing; **16.** Berlin; **17.** Salzburg; **18.** Cape Town. *Famous landmark:* Great Pyramid of Giza.

51.   Hiding in plain sight: 1. Vietnam/Etna; **2.** Finland/inland; **3.** Botswana/swan; **4.** Rwanda/wand; **5.** Netherlands/ether; **6.** Philippines/pine; **7.** Madagascar/scar;

8. Bangladesh/glades; **9.** Germany/many; **10.** Maldives/dives; **11.** Slovenia/love; **12.** Micronesia/crones; **13.** North Macedonia/mace; **14.** Spain/pain; **15.** Ireland or Iceland/eland; **16.** Bulgaria/aria; **17.** Palestine/palest; **18.** Singapore/pore; **19.** Thailand/hail; **20.** Sweden/swede; **21.** Kuwait/wait; **22.** Indonesia/done; **23.** Romania/mania; **24.** New Zealand/zeal; **25.** Denmark/mark.

52.   Masai Mara:

53.   In good faith: 1. Notre-Dame de Paris; **2.** Westminster Abbey; **3.** Istanbul, Turkey; **4.** it is built into a steep rocky hillside; **5.** Canterbury Cathedral (officially the Cathedral and Metropolitical Church of Christ at Canterbury); **6.** Great Mosque of Mecca (al-Masjid al-Ḥarām), Saudi Arabia; **7.** Venice, Italy; **8.** Blue Mosque; **9.** Sagrada Família, Barcelona; **10.** Angkor Wat; **11.** Jerusalem; **12.** The Cardboard Cathedral (the roof design incorporates nearly a hundred giant cardboard tubes, 20m/65 ft in length); **13.** Hungary; **14.** St Peter's Basilica (Basilica Papale di San Pietro); **15.** India; **16.** Moscow; **17.** Church (or

Basilica) of the Nativity; **18.** Indonesia (on the island of Java); **19.** a network of ancient pilgrimage routes; **20.** Brazil.

54. **Flying the flag: 1.** K (Japan); **2.** D (Liberia); **3.** B (Cuba); **4.** A (Canada); **5.** E (Tunisia); **6.** H (Seychelles); **7.** L (Australia); **8.** C (Brazil); **9.** J (South Korea); **10.** I (Georgia); **11.** G (South Africa); **12.** F (Greece).

55. **Dressed to kill: 1.** Japan; **2.** fez; **3.** South America; **4.** lederhosen; **5.** Vietnam; **6.** on your head (it's a knitted bonnet); **7.** sari (or saree/sharee); **8.** clogs; **9.** New Zealand; **10.** niqab; **11.** sombrero; **12.** huipil.

56. **Island in the Sun: 1.** Baffin Island/Canada; **2.** Capri/Italy; **3.** Corfu/Greece; **4.** Floreana Island/Ecuador; **5.** Fraser Island/Australia; **6.** Great Barrier Island/New Zealand; **7.** Hokkaido/Japan; **8.** Java/Indonesia; **9.** La Gomera/Spain; **10.** New Britain/Papua New Guinea; **11.** Nosy Be/Madagascar; **12.** Qeshm Island/Iran; **13.** Réunion/France; **14.** Robinson Crusoe Island/Chile; **15.** Saaranpaskantamasaari/Finland; **16.** Sal/Cape Verde; **17.** Socotra/Yemen; **18.** Spitsbergen/Norway; **19.** Streymoy/Denmark; **20.** Tresco/United Kingdom.

57. **Twist of fate: 1.** Tennessee; **2.** Edinburgh; **3.** Hindustani; **4.** Islamophobic; **5.** Cambridge; **6.** Ecuadorian; **7.** Nepal; **8.** Lamborghini; **9.** iguanas; **10.** sandstone; **11.** escargot; **12.** Tanzanian. *Anagram:* Liechtenstein.

58. **Mental map: 1.** Lake Ontario; **2.** Brazil, Colombia and Ecuador; **3.** Austria and Lichtenstein; **4.** Madagascar (after 6,700km/4,150 miles); **5.** Gianna's is the longest journey (1,420km), then Martina's (1,270km), then Lukas's (1,060km); **6.** Bolivia; **7.** Two (Bulgaria and Romania); **8.** Iran; **9.** six (USA, Mexico, Guatemala, Honduras, Nicaragua and Costa Rica); **10.** Buenos Aires; **11.** Brisbane; **12.** Bratislava (Slovakia); **13.** Sicily; **14.** Malta; **15.** Romania and Ukraine; **16.** Saudi Arabia; **17.** China and India; **18.** the Moscow flight arrives first as it has 4,350km (2,700 miles) to travel, compared to 5,850km (3,630 miles) for the plane coming from Tokyo; **19.** Morocco, Algeria, Tunisia, Libya, Egypt; **20.** Tunisia; **21.** Chile; **22.** Russia; **23.** Portugal; **24.** Algeria and DR Congo; **25.** Greenland.

59. **Know your onions: 1.** A; **2.** H; **3.** B; **4.** D; **5.** G; **6.** I; **7.** F; **8.** C; **9.** E; **10.** K; **11.** L; **12.** J.

60. **Pirates of the Caribbean: 1.** Cuba; **2.** Kingston; **3.** Trinidad and Tobago; **4.** they are all self-governing British Overseas Territories; **5.** The Bahamas; **6.** Saint Lucia; **7.** Curaçao; **8.** Barbados; **9.** *Our Man in Havana*; **10.** pigs; **11.** Suriname; **12.** Montserrat.

61. **Go with the flow: 1.** Rhine; **2.** Thames (Thames Path National Trail); **3.** Nile; **4.** Colorado; **5.** Danube; **6.** Seine; **7.** Hudson; **8.** Murray; **9.** Severn; **10.** Mississippi; **11.** Po; **12.** Zambezi; **13.** Volga; **14.** Yangtze; **15.** a channel or valley that is usually dry but flows like a river after heavy rain; **16.** Amazon; **17.** hippopotamus; **18.** Ganges; **19.** Yukon (UConn); **20.** Thailand; **21.** Blue Nile and White Nile; **22.** Orange; **23.** Iraq; **24.** Tunisia (it has just one permanent river, the Medjerda, whereas the

other countries have none); **25.** Tiber (known locally as Tevere).

62. **A novel setting: 1.** M (Russia); **2.** B (Canada); **3.** I (Sweden); **4.** H (Nigeria); **5.** O (China); **6.** A (Mexico); **7.** G (United Kingdom); **8.** C (Cuba); **9.** L (Afghanistan); **10.** D (Colombia); **11.** K (Botswana); **12.** P (Australia); **13.** E (Brazil); **14.** N (India); **15.** J (Lithuania); **16.** F (Spain).

63. **All fun and games: 1.** Summer 2016/ Rio de Janeiro; **2.** Winter 2014/Sochi; **3.** Summer 2012/London; **4.** Winter 2010/Vancouver; **5.** Summer 2008/ Beijing; **6.** Winter 2006/Turin; **7.** Summer 2004/Athens; **8.** Winter 2002/Salt Lake City; **9.** Summer 2000/ Sydney; **10.** Summer 1996/Atlanta; **11.** Summer 1988/Seoul; **12.** Winter 1984/Sarajevo; **13.** Winter 1964/ Innsbruck; **14.** Summer 1936/Berlin; **15.** Summer 1900/Paris.

64. **Capital gains: 1.** International Monetary Fund; **2.** Petroleum (Organisation of Petroleum Exporting Countries); **3.** Educational, Scientific and Cultural; **4.** Self-Contained Underwater Breathing Apparatus; **5.** Atlantic (North Atlantic Treaty Organisation); **6.** You Only Live Once; **7.** International and Emergency; **8.** Zimbabwe (Zimbabwe African National Union – Patriotic Front); **9.** Subscriber Identification Module; **10.** USSR (Union of Soviet Socialist Republics); **11.** SNCF; **12.** African National Congress; **13.** Kuala Lumpur; **14.** ICBM (Inter-Continental Ballistic Missile – the others are: International Olympic Committee, International Standard Book Number, International Space Station, and International Union for Conservation of Nature); **15.** Former Yugoslav Republic.

65. **World knowledge:** *Across:* **1.** scribes; **5.** totem; **8.** canal; **9.** capital; **10.** bus; **11.** Venezuela; **12.** yogurt; **14.** Odessa; **18.** Mauritius; **20.** rue; **21.** chancel; **22.** India; **23.** Ashes; **24.** Nairobi. *Down:* **1.** sickbay; **2.** runes; **3.** bolivar; **4.** second; **5.** topaz; **6.** tethers; **7.** Malta; **13.** goulash; **15.** dashiki; **16.** Abenaki; **17.** violin; **18.** Mecca; **19.** Incas; **20.** rodeo.

66. **Knocked for six: 1.** Dublin; **2.** shekel; **3.** Bhutan; **4.** trifle; **5.** France; **6.** Russia (.su was assigned before the Soviet Union was dissolved and is still used in parallel with .ru); **7.** Alaska; **8.** Jordan; **9.** Madrid; **10.** Rwanda; **11.** Cyprus; **12.** Amstel; **13.** Shinto; **14.** Kuwait; **15.** Greece.

67. **The American dream: 1.** C; **2.** P; **3.** K; **4.** L; **5.** J; **6.** E; **7.** D; **8.** I; **9.** H; **10.** M; **11.** G; **12.** N; **13.** A; **14.** B; **15.** O; **16.** F; **17.** Q; **18.** T; **19.** S; **20.** R.

68. **Facts and figures: 1.** G; **2.** D; **3.** H; **4.** J; **5.** C; **6.** F; **7.** E; **8.** B; **9.** I; **10.** A.

69. **Tour...nado!** Jed/Nightlife/£100/ Sunhat; Jen/Volcanoes/£200/ Toothbrush; Jill/Meditation/£400/ Credit card; Jim/Birding/£300/ Underwear; Jon/Monuments/£500/ Camera.

70. **Face the music: 1.** Bangkok; **2.** Ethiopia; **3.** Egyptian; **4.** Rotterdam; **5.** London; **6.** Japan; **7.** San José; **8.** Ibiza; **9.** San Francisco; **10.** Norwegian; **11.** Moscow; **12.** Paris.

71. **Endemic creatures: 1.** Aldabra giant tortoise/Seychelles; **2.** Amami rabbit/ Japan; **3.** Asiatic lion/India; **4.** aye- aye/Madagascar; **5.** gelada/Ethiopia; **6.** giant panda/China; **7.** golden lion tamarin/Brazil; **8.** Indus river dolphin/ Pakistan; **9.** kakapo/New Zealand; **10.** Komodo dragon/Indonesia;

11. marine iguana/Galápagos;
12. proboscis monkey/Borneo;
13. tree lobster/Lord Howe Islands;
14. vaquita/Mexico; **15.** wombat/
Australia.

72. On the dot:

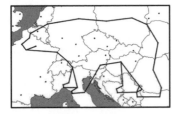

73. Mind your language:
1. Maltese; **2.** Spanish; **3.** French;
4. German; **5.** Kirundi; **6.** Catalan;
7. Hebrew; **8.** Burmese; **9.** Italian;
10. Tok Pisin; **11.** Arabic;
12. Mandarin; **13.** English;
14. Malagasy; **15.** Punjabi; **16.** Hindi;
17. Portuguese; **18.** Lao. *Travel advice:*
speak the local lingo.

74. Industrial strength: 1. bananas/
India; **2.** cars/China; **3.** cashew
nuts/Vietnam; **4.** cherries/Turkey;
5. cocoa/Ivory Coast; **6.** coffee/Brazil;
7. daffodils/United Kingdom; **8.** digital
cameras/Japan; **9.** military weaponry/
USA; **10.** oats/Russia; **11.** olives/
Spain; **12.** palm oil/Indonesia;
13. rubber/Thailand; **14.** saffron/
Iran; **15.** sunflower seeds/Ukraine;
16. tulips/Netherlands; **17.** vanilla/
Madagascar; **18.** wool/Australia.

75. A lot in common: 1. Zambia and
Zimbabwe; **2.** Iraq and Iran; **3.** Latvia
and Lithuania; **4.** Malawi and
Mozambique or Mali and Mauritania;
5. Nigeria and Niger; **6.** Eritrea
and Ethiopia; **7.** Kazakhstan and
Kyrgyzstan; **8.** Benin and Burkina Faso
or Bolivia and Brazil; **9.** Armenia and
Azerbaijan; **10.** Cameroon, Central

African Republic and Chad.

76. Landmarks of the East: 1. L/
Sydney Opera House (Australia); **2.** G/
Taj Mahal (Agra, India); **3.** B/Abu
Simbel temples (Nubia, Egypt); **4.** I/
Tokyo Tower (Japan); **5.** A/Nelson
Mandela Capture Site (Howick, South
Africa); **6.** J/Angkor Wat (Siem Reap,
Cambodia); **7.** K/Petronas Towers
(Kuala Lumpur, Malaysia); **8.** F/Burj Al
Arab (Dubai, United Arab Emirates);
9. H/Temple of Heaven (Beijing,
China); **10.** D/Al-Shaheed Monument
or Martyr's Memorial (Baghdad, Iraq);
11. C/Galata Tower (Istanbul, Turkey);
12. E/Azadi Tower, formerly Shahyad
Tower (Tehran, Iran).

77. Right on the money: 1. Deutsche
Mark; **2.** loonie (in reference to the
common loon; French-speaking
Canadians refer to the coin as 'huard'
for the same reason); **3.** Czech
Republic; **4.** British pound; **5.** kwacha;
6. dinar; **7.** Australia (Australian
dollar); **8.** Vietnam; **9.** Kenya, Somalia,
Somaliland, Tanzania or Uganda;
10. Turkey (lira) – Syria and Lebanon
are also arguably acceptable answers,
as they also refer to their currencies
as 'lira' in Arabic, although officially
in English these are called the
Syrian pound and Lebanese pound;
11. won; **12.** Brazil; **13.** Japanese
yen; **14.** Malaysia (ringgit); **15.** Cape
Verde; **16.** Indian rupee; **17.** China;
18. baht (subdivided into 100
satang); **19.** Poland; **20.** they are all
called 'pound'; **21.** peso (Argentina,
Chile, Colombia, Uruguay); **22.** euro;
23. Hungary; **24.** Australia; **25.** Queen
Elizabeth II.

78. All roads lead to Rome: 1. Alitalia;
2. Galicia (it's in Spain); **3.** appetisers/
starters; **4.** Austria; **5.** Michelangelo;

6. moped; **7.** San Marino; **8.** Trevi Fountain; **9.** Genoa; **10.** Mazzanti (it's an Italian high-performance car manufacturer); **11.** Spanish Steps; **12.** Silvio Berlusconi; **13.** Venice; **14.** telemea (it's Romanian); **15.** Palermo (on Sicily).

79. **High and mighty:** Alps, Altai, Annapurna, Apennines, Atlas, Eiger, Elbrus, El Capitan, Etna, Fuji, Jura, Makalu, Mauna Kea, Olympus, Robson, Snowdon, Taurus, Tien Shan, Uludağ, Urals.

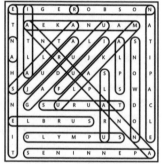

80. **Dear Old Blighty: 1.** Kew Gardens; **2.** M25; **3.** Anglesey; **4.** all had a 'Royal' prefix bestowed upon them by the monarch (in 1838, 1909 and 2011 respectively); **5.** Wales (it was considered part of England when the flag was designed); **6.** Lord High Chancellor of Great Britain (this office is held by a cabinet minister); **7.** Great Britain refers to the large island comprising England, Scotland and Wales, while the United Kingdom is the country comprising not just Great Britain but also Northern Ireland; **8.** Tower of London; **9.** Hereford Cow-Painting Festival; **10.** Thistle; **11.** Stratford-upon-Avon; **12.** Inverness; **13.** Bodleian Library; **14.** Wembley Stadium; **15.** doctors/

surgeons; **16.** journalists; **17.** tailors; **18.** Manchester; **19.** city of dreaming spires; **20.** Stormont; **21.** Glasgow; **22.** St David; **23.** cabbage; **24.** George VI; **25.** Platform 9¾.

81. **Come rain or shine: 1.** Glasgow (112cm); **2.** London (56cm); **3.** Réunion; **4.** local winds; **5.** Trondheim (the others are all north of the Arctic Circle); **6.** aurora australis; **7.** it was reversed (water boiled at 0°C and froze at 100°C); **8.** Tel Aviv (3,311hrs); **9.** Tokyo (1,872hrs); **10.** 160,000; **11.** Richter magnitude scale; **12.** Beaufort wind force scale; **13.** Darwin (27.6°C/ 81.7°F); **14.** Nairobi (17.8°C/ 64.0°F); **15.** monsoon; **16.** a type of duststorm or sandstorm; **17.** thunder and lightning (later versions of the poem were printed with their names changed to the German 'Donner and Blitzen'); **18.** an earthquake; **19.** avalanches; **20.** flooding; **21.** dam failure; **22.** a hailstorm; **23.** typhoon; **24.** Louisiana; **25.** 26 December (it's often called the Boxing Day Tsunami).

82. **Gone walkabout: 1.** E; **2.** C; **3.** K; **4.** F; **5.** I; **6.** B; **7.** L; **8.** H; **9.** D; **10.** G; **11.** A; **12.** J.

83. **Fair and square: 1.** flowers (specifically begonias); **2.** Trafalgar Square, London; **3.** China; **4.** Red Square, Moscow; **5.** St Peter's Square (Piazza San Pietro); **6.** Times Square, New York; **7.** Berlin; **8.** Wenceslas Square; 9, Budapest, Hungary; **10.** Bogotá, Colombia.

84. **Windmills of Your Mind: 1.** Iceland; **2.** Denmark; **3.** Kabul; **4.** landlocked; **5.** dictatorship; **6.** Pompidou; **7.** Uruguay; **8.** yurt; **9.** Titanic; **10.** chinstrap; **11.** Portugal; **12.** Laos; **13.** Skopje; **14.** Europol; **15.** Lima;

16. Arab; **17.** Baku. *Anagram:* duck-billed platypus.

85. Like herding cats: 1. D; **2.** F; **3.** A; **4.** H; **5.** E; **6.** B; **7.** G; **8.** C.

86. Irritable vowel syndrome:
1. Reykjavik (Iceland); **2.** London (United Kingdom); **3.** Rome (Italy); **4.** Canberra (Australia); **5.** Cairo (Egypt); **6.** Tallinn (Estonia); **7.** Doha (Qatar); **8.** Nairobi (Kenya); **9.** Ankara (Turkey); **10.** Antananarivo (Madagascar); **11.** Santiago (Chile); **12.** Islamabad (Pakistan); **13.** Tehran (Iran); **14.** Oslo (Norway); **15.** Athens (Greece); **16.** Ottawa (Canada); **17.** Apia (Samoa); **18.** Ouagadougou (Burkina Faso).

87. Joy to the World: 1. Germany; **2.** seven swans a-swimming; **3.** Norway; **4.** Krampus; **5.** Noël; **6.** Turkey; **7.** *Hark! The Herald Angels Sing;* **8.** junkanoo or jonkonnu; **9.** goat; **10.** *Good King Wenceslas.*

88. Armchair traveller: 1. E (*On the Road*); **2.** D (*Round Ireland with a Fridge*); **3.** I (*Coasting*); **4.** B (*In Patagonia*); **5.** F (*Venice*); **6.** H (*A Short Walk in the Hindu Kush*); **7.** G (*Full Tilt: Ireland to India with a Bicycle*); **8.** A (*Notes From a Small Island*); **9.** J (*The Great Railway Bazaar: By Train Through Asia*); **10.** C (*Eat, Pray, Love: One Woman's Search for Everything Across Italy, India and Indonesia*).

89. Stan-ding out from the crowd:
Kazakhstan/Brummell & Oleynik/Nur-Sultan/2,725,000km²; Kyrgyzstan/Mitchell/Bishkek/200,000km²; Tajikistan/Ibbotson & Lovell-Hoare/Dushanbe/143,000km²; Turkmenistan/Brummell/Ashgabat/491,000km²; Uzbekistan/Ibbotson & Burford/Tashkent/448,000km².

90. Fickle finger of fate: 1. flamenco; **2.** Finland; **3.** Faroe Islands; **4.** France; **5.** Fort Knox; **6.** Forbidden City; **7.** forest; **8.** Flying Fish Cove; **9.** Founding Fathers (of the United States); **10.** Flemish; **11.** Radamel Falcao; **12.** franc; **13.** French 75; **14.** Fiji (typographically, a tittle is the dot on a lowercase i or j); **15.** Footprint Travel Guides.

91. A flying start: 1. Ben Gurion/Tel Aviv, Israel; **2.** Charles de Gaulle/Paris, France; **3.** David the Builder/Kutaisi, Georgia; **4.** El Dorado/Bogotá, Colombia; **5.** Gatwick/London, UK; **6.** Incheon/Seoul, South Korea; **7.** John Lennon/Liverpool, UK; **8.** John Paul II/Kraków, Poland; **9.** King Shaka/Durban, South Africa; **10.** Marco Polo/Venice, Italy; **11.** Mohammed V/Casablanca, Morocco; **12.** O'Hare/Chicago, USA; **13.** Schiphol/Amsterdam, Netherlands; **14.** Thunder Bay/Ontario, Canada; **15.** Vnukovo/Moscow, Russia.

92. Movers and shakers: 1. Sweden; **2.** Egypt; **3.** Italy; **4.** New Zealand; **5.** Denmark; **6.** South Africa; **7.** Belgium; **8.** Greece; **9.** Poland; **10.** Brazil; **11.** Czech Republic; **12.** Ukraine; **13.** Israel; **14.** United Kingdom; **15.** Mexico; **16.** France; **17.** Tanzania; **18.** Yemen.

93. World leaders: *Across:* **7.** Jacques Chirac; **8.** idea; **9.** Sardinia; **10.** empire; **12.** body; **13.** RTE; **14.** July; **15.** Reagan; **16.** tsarinas/csarinas; **19.** Rudd; **20.** Middle Eastern. *Down:* **1.** Saddam Hussein; **2.** equality; **3.** Hess; **4.** Schröder; **5.** Bibi; **6.** Jacinda Ardern; **11.** Erlander; **12.** Blairite; **17.** Rudi; **18.** shah.

94. A head for heights: 1. E; **2.** K; **3.** I; **4.** P; **5.** H; **6.** G; **7.** J; **8.** T (or 46m/151 ft without the plinth); **9.** M; **10.** D; **11.** A; **12.** N; **13.** O; **14.** Q; **15.** F; **16.** L; **17.** R; **18.** C (Mont Blanc); **19.** B; **20.** S (K2).

95. I'll drink to that! 1. Brazil; **2.** Czech Republic (with an annual consumption of 192 litres, compared to 108 litres by Austria in second place); **3.** milk; **4.** Spain and Portugal; **5.** anise; **6.** South Korea (or Korea, as the drink predates the country's split); **7.** aiuto (it is Italian for 'help!' – the others are Afrikaans, Czech, German, Spanish, French and Scandinavian respectively); **8.** Mexico; **9.** Iceland; **10.** mojito; **11.** New Zealand; **12.** yoghurt; **13.** Pimm's (specifically Pimm's No 1 Cup); **14.** South Africa.

96. New World order: 1. F; **2.** E; **3.** H; **4.** C; **5.** B; **6.** D; **7.** G; **8.** A; **9.** K; **10.** R; **11.** L; **12.** O; **13.** J; **14.** U; **15.** M; **16.** P; **17.** N; **18.** T;**19.** S; **20.** V; **21.** I; **22.** Q; **23.** X; **24.** Z; **25.** W; **26.** Y.

97. Barking up the wrong tree: 1. Sherwood Forest; **2.** maple (*Acer*); **3.** Japan; **4.** pineapples; **5.** Brazil; **6.** monkey puzzle; **7.** Black Forest; **8.** Madagascar; **9.** oak; **10.** cotton (it grows on a flowering plant 1m/3 ft or so in height); **11.** Russia; **12.** sequoia (also called coast redwood, *Sequoia sempervirens*); **13.** turpentine; **14.** Asia; **15.** gum; **16.** Stereophonics; **17.** China; **18.** peanuts (they grow underground); **19.** Morocco; **20.** Brazil; **21.** balsa; **22.** Lebanon; **23.** horse chestnut (*Aesculus*); **24.** dendrology (astacology is the study of crayfish, campanology is the art of bellringing, deltiology is the collection of postcards, selenology is the study of the Moon, and trichology is the branch of dermatology concerned with scalp health);

25. dragon's blood tree (*Dracaena cinnabari*).

98. Napa Valley:

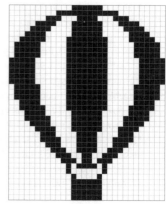

99. Oddballs: 1. They're all places in Australia except Auckland (New Zealand); **2.** They all share a border with Switzerland except Hungary; **3.** They're all red, white and blue except the German flag (black, red and yellow); **4.** They're all birds except mountain chicken (a large Caribbean frog); **5.** They're all island countries except Vietnam; **6.** They're all Swedish except Nokia (Finnish); **7.** They're all places in the United Kingdom except Bilbao (in Spain); **8.** They've all had airports named in their honour except David Beckham; **9.** They're all in the GMT time zone except Peru (5 hours behind GMT); **10.** They're all animals with misleading names except polar bears, which genuinely *are* bears (Bombay ducks are fish, electric eels are knifefish, flying foxes are bats, flying lemurs are colugos, guinea pigs are rodents, killer whales are dolphins, king cobras are in a separate genus from true cobras, koala bears are marsupials, maned wolves are only distantly related to wolves, prairie dogs are rodents, and red pandas are the sole species in a family more closely related to seals than pandas); **11.** They're all names of large lakes (among the world's top 20) except Paris; **12.** The equator passes through all of them except India; **13.** They're all sharks except panda; **14.** They're all recent US First Ladies except Carla (which was the name of the wife of French president Nicolas Sarkozy); **15.** They're all stringed instruments, played with a bow except bougarabou (a type of drum); **16.** They're all country names in reverse apart from Esrever (which is 'reverse' in reverse).

100. **Alphabet soup: 1.** Austria; **2.** Bolivia; **3.** Chad; **4.** Danube; **5.** Euphrates; **6.** funicular; **7.** Georgia; **8.** Hormuz; **9.** Iguazu; **10.** Jordan; **11.** kakapo; **12.** Lufthansa; **13.** Mississippi; **14.** Nepal; **15.** Olympus; **16.** Paris; **17.** Quebec; **18.** Rand; **19.** Saskatchewan; **20.** Turkey; **21.** Uluru; **22.** Venezuela; **23.** Wellington; **24.** xerophytic; **25.** Yosemite; **26.** Zócalo.

101. **Arabian nights: 1.** D; **2.** B; **3.** G; **4.** K; **5.** I; **6.** A; **7.** F; **8.** C; **9.** L; **10.** E; **11.** J; **12.** H.

102. **A Room with A View: 1.** Waldorf salad (named for the Waldorf Hotel, now called the Waldorf–Astoria); **2.** Kenya; **3.** Torquay; **4.** it is made of ice (and has to be rebuilt every year); **5.** North Korea; **6.** *Hotel California*; **7.** Memphis, Tennessee; **8.** Singapore; **9.** an aeroplane (Boeing 727); **10.** The Savoy (on Savoy Court); **11.** *The Best Exotic Marigold Hotel*; **12.** Berlin, Germany (Hotel Adlon Kempinski).

103. **Deep and meaningful: 1.** Japan; **2.** Philippines; **3.** El Salvador; **4.** Cyprus; **5.** Belarus; **6.** Eritrea;

7. Venezuela; **8.** hippopotamus; **9.** silver; **10.** Australia; **11.** they all take their names from rivers; **12.** shrimps; **13.** Spain; **14.** village; **15.** Comoros.

104. **It's all Greek to me: 1.** Thailand (it says 'Bangkok'); **2.** Georgia (it says 'bon voyage'); **3.** B; **4.** D; **5.** C; **6.** A (all four of the texts A–D are transcriptions of the name 'Donald Trump'); **7.** Greek (it says 'Greek alphabet'); **8.** Cyrillic (the sample text is the opening line of Tolstoy's *Anna Karenina* – 'Happy families are all alike; every unhappy family is unhappy in its own way.'); **9.** Arabic (it is pronounced as *rouhi wa rouhoki ya rouhi rouhain be rouhen, matrah ma tarouho rouhoka rouhi betrouh*, meaning 'my soul and your soul are one soul; wherever your soul goes, my soul goes too'); **10.** Hebrew; **11.** Leonardo DiCaprio (in Russian); **12.** Kim Kardashian (in Greek); **13.** Steven Spielberg (in the International Phonetic Alphabet); **14.** Angelina Jolie (in Russian); **15.** Cher (in Morse Code); **16.** Barrack Obama (in Greek); **17.** Vladimir Putin (in Braille); **18.** Madonna (in Persian); **19.** Egyptian hieroglyphs or hieroglyphics (it says 'naked man'); **20.** Algeria, Libya, Mali, Morocco, Niger or Tunisia (it says 'Is there someone here who speaks English?'); **21.** Inuktitut; **22.** Austrian (a sneaky question as, of course, this is not a language script at all but mathematical notation – it is Schrödinger's equation, the most fundamental equation in quantum mechanics, which he first published in 1926 and which is inscribed on his gravestone).

105. **From here to Timbuktu: 1.** Mali; **2.** Johannesburg (O R Tambo International Airport); **3.** Kenya;

4. Mozambique; **5.** Tanzania; **6.** Two – Zambia and Tanzania; **7.** Two – the white (or square-lipped) rhino and the black (or hook-lipped) rhino; **8.** Sahara, Kalahari and Namib; **9.** Uganda; **10.** Mount Kilimanjaro (of which Kibo is the highest peak); **11.** You would still be in Algeria! **12.** Nigeria.

106. Points of reference: 1. M; **2.** H; **3.** G; **4.** A; **5.** C; **6.** E; **7.** B; **8.** N; **9.** D; **10.** I; **11.** L; **12.** K; **13.** F; **14.** J.

107. Paint the town red: 1. Oktoberfest (known locally as d'Wiesn); **2.** Thailand; **3.** cherry blossom; **4.** Mexico; **5.** tomatoes; **6.** oranges; **7.** orange; **8.** India; **9.** running of the bulls (known locally as encierro); **10.** Scotland, UK; **11.** Holi; **12.** China; **13.** the race's distance of 500 miles; **14.** March (17th); **15.** Venice, Italy; **16.** São Paulo, Brazil; **17.** Iditarod Trail; **18.** Singapore; **19.** Nevada; **20.** mud.

108. City skylines: 1. Singapore; **2.** Tokyo, Japan; **3.** Sydney, Australia; **4.** Dubai, United Arab Emirates; **5.** Rio de Janeiro, Brazil; **6.** Paris, France; **7.** Taipei, Taiwan; **8.** Vancouver, Canada.

109. Bones of contention: 1. Gibraltar; **2.** Kosovo (officially the Autonomous Province of Kosovo and Metohija); **3.** Crimea; **4.** Western Sahara; **5.** Mont Blanc (and the nearby Dôme du Goûter); **6.** Korean Peninsula; **7.** Mayotte; **8.** Japan; **9.** Antarctica; **10.** Kashmir.

110. Every dog has his day: 1. Barak Hound/Bosnia & Herzegovina; **2.** Basenji/DR Congo; **3.** Chihuahua/Mexico; **4.** Chinook/USA; **5.** Dalmatian/Croatia; **6.** Great Dane/Germany; **7.** Kangal Shepherd Dog/Turkey; **8.** Karelian Bear Dog/Finland;

9. Koolie/Australia; **10.** Newfoundland/Canada; **11.** Picardy Spaniel/France; **12.** Pug/China; **13.** Puli/Hungary; **14.** Red Setter/Ireland; **15.** Samoyed/Russia; **16.** Serrano Bulldog/Brazil; **17.** Shih Tzu/Tibet; **18.** Whippet/United Kingdom.

111. Screen test: 1. Australia; **2.** Thailand; **3.** Russia; **4.** Belgium; **5.** Canada; **6.** Mexico; **7.** Greece; **8.** Germany; **9.** Argentina; **10.** Ireland; **11.** Italy; **12.** India; **13.** Norway; **14.** Japan; **15.** Austria; **16.** Spain; **17.** France; **18.** Egypt.; *Film title: Slumdog Millionaire.*

112. Where am I? 1. Greece; **2.** Brazil; **3.** Jamaica; **4.** Egypt; **5.** Vietnam; **6.** Iceland; **7.** Turkey; **8.** Japan; **9.** Mexico; **10.** New Zealand.

113. Straight and narrow: 1. Chile; **2.** Norway; **3.** The Gambia; **4.** Cuba; **5.** Vietnam; **6.** Japan; **7.** Israel; **8.** New Zealand.

114. Tiny Tim's treasure trove: 1. Tower Bridge; **2.** Tallinn; **3.** tortillas; **4.** Tunisia; **5.** Tiananmen Square; **6.** Tutankhamun; **7.** (Leo) Tolstoy; **8.** tarantella; **9.** Tranmere Rovers; **10.** Tuareg people (also spelled Twareg or Touareg); **11.** Tallahassee; **12.** Tudors; **13.** Toblerone; **14.** Lake Tanganyika; **15.** (Alan) Turing.

115. Megacities: 1. K; **2.** C; **3.** L; **4.** N; **5.** H; **6.** J; **7.** B; **8.** E; **9.** I; **10.** M; **11.** G; **12.** A.

116. Uncle Sam: 1. Texas; **2.** Kansas and Kentucky; **3.** Oregon; **4.** Maryland; **5.** Minnesota; **6.** Florida; **7.** Alabama; **8.** California; **9.** Arizona; **10.** Iowa, Ohio and Utah; **11.** North Carolina; **12.** Florida; **13.** Pennsylvania; **14.** Wyoming; **15.** Colorado, North Carolina, Oregon, Delaware; **16.** Hawaii; **17.** Eastern Standard

Time; **18.** Mountain Standard Time;
19. yellowhammer (also called
northern flicker or common flicker);
20. Massachusetts, North Dakota,
Arkansas, Indiana; **21.** Kentucky;
22. Maine; **23.** Austin; **24.** Kansas;
25. none; **26.** Colorado; **27.** New
Mexico; **28.** Alaska; **29.** Maine,
Missouri, Rhode Island, Alabama;
30. Gulf of Mexico; **31.** Hawaii;
32. Wisconsin; **33.** South Carolina;
34. Arkansas; **35.** brown bear
(specifically the now-extinct California
grizzly bear).

117. In a spin: 1. Belize; **2.** Everest;
3. Tuvalu; **4.** Ukraine; **5.** Ethiopia;
6. Athens; **7.** Sahara; **8.** Ankara;
9. Assisi; **10.** Ireland; **11.** dram;
12. Madagascar; **13.** Russian;
14. Nairobi; **15.** Inuktitut; **16.** tiger;
17. reggae. *Anagram*: United Arab
Emirates.

118. A drop in the ocean: 1. D; **2.** C; **3.** H;
4. N; **5.** B; **6.** E; **7.** A; **8.** L; **9.** K; **10.** J;
11. M; **12.** F; **13.** I; **14.** G.

119. Tower of Babel: 1. Arabic; **2.** Spanish;
3. Afrikaans; **4.** Nahuatl; **5.** Hindi;
6. Russian; **7.** Italian; **8.** Malay;
9. Turkish; **10.** Dutch; **11.** French;
12. Hawaiian; **13.** Japanese;
14. Cantonese; **15.** Czech;
16. German.

120. Flights of fancy: 1. Dubai
International Airport; **2.** repeated
sightings of a drone near the runway;
3. LAX; **4.** Kenya Airways; **5.** India;
6. it is a beach and can only be used
at low tide; **7.** Japan; **8.** all are built
next to international borders and have
direct entrances from both countries;
9. Las Vegas; **10.** Emirates; **11.** Atlanta
Airport (officially Hartsfield–Jackson
Atlanta International Airport);
12. they are built on artificial

islands; **13.** Boeing 787; **14.** EasyJet;
15. Germany; **16.** Bangkok, Thailand;
17. to enable the emergency
evacuation slide on their designated
exit then double-check that their
colleague on the opposite side
of the aircraft has done the same;
18. Barcelona, Spain; **19.** Canada;
20. four (Terminal 1 closed down in
2015; the operational terminals are
numbered 2 to 5); **21.** an 18-hole
golf course; **22.** KLM Royal Dutch
Airlines; **23.** they are among a small
number of IATA codes that do not
refer to specific airports but to a group
of multiple airports serving one city;
24. Russia (at Zhukovsky International
Airport, Moscow); **25.** they all have
runways with level crossings (the
Gibraltar runway is crossed by a
major public road, while those at
Gisborne and Manakara are crossed
by railways).

121. Brand loyalty: 1. N; **2.** O; **3.** D; **4.** T;
5. R; **6.** F; **7.** K; **8.** G; **9.** E; **10.** P; **11.** M;
12. J; **13.** L; **14.** Q; **15.** U; **16.** H; **17.** I;
18. A; **19.** B; **20.** C; **21.** S.

122. Mark my words: 1. lost; **2.** footprints;
3. single step; **4.** only a page;
5. regrets; **6.** at home; **7.** friends;
8. trips take people; **9.** undreamed;
10. comfort zone; **11.** eyes; **12.** my
diary; **13.** tiny place; **14.** routine;
15. Tourists / travellers; **16.** remember
more than I have seen; **17.** do not
love; **18.** control; **19.** everyone is
wrong; **20.** emotions; **21.** world is
wide; **22.** foreign lands / foreign;
23. on my list; **24.** half the clothes
/ twice the money; **25.** hat keeps
blowing off.

123. Ain't No Mountain High Enough:
1. approximately 10 times (Burj
Khalifa is 830m; Mount Everest is

8,848m); **2.** Mont Blanc; **3.** The Andes; **4.** Denali; **5.** The Urals; **6.** New Zealand; **7.** The Caucasus; **8.** Andorra; **9.** K2 (also called Chhogori or Mount Godwin-Austen); **10.** Egypt; **11.** Jurassic Period (after Jura Mountains); **12.** Atlas Mountains; **13.** Israel; **14.** The Matterhorn; **15.** Slovakia; **16.** Mount Everest Base Camp; **17.** Mexico; **18.** USA (Alaska).

124. Walk on the Wild Side: buffalo, bush baby, bush pig, eland, elephant, gemsbok, giraffe, gorilla, hyena, hyrax, impala, kudu, leopard, lion, monkey, okapi, rhino, snake, vulture, zebra.

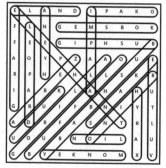

125. A pair of clues: 1 & 40. Georgia; **2 & 28.** Amazon; **3 & 33.** Madagascar; **4 & 37.** China; **5 & 23.** Casablanca; **6 & 25.** Shiraz; **7 & 34.** Graceland; **8 & 35.** Waterloo; **9 & 31.** Bush; **10 & 30.** Turkey; **11 & 29.** Swede; **12 & 38.** Stilton; **13 & 22.** kiwi; **14 & 24.** Darwin; **15 & 39.** ash; **16 & 21.** Brazil; **17 & 36.** Wellington; **18 & 32.** Kiev; **19 & 27.** Victoria; **20 & 26.** Sofia.

126. Trip of a lifetime: Alex/Machu Picchu/2011/16 days; Greg/Acropolis (Athens)/2008/20 days; Lou/Victoria Falls/2014/18 days; Mel/Grand Canyon/2013/12 days; Val/Galápagos/2009/10 days.

127. Rise and fall of the Roman Empire: 1. Andautonia/Zagreb; **2.** Aquae Sulis/Bath; **3.** Aquincum/Budapest; **4.** Argentoratum/Strasbourg; **5.** Londinium/London; **6.** Lugdunum/Lyon; **7.** Lutetia/Paris; **8.** Mamucium/Manchester; **9.** Massilia/Marseille; **10.** Neapolis/Naples; **11.** Nida/Frankfurt; **12.** Ragusium/Dubrovnik; **13.** Turicum/Zurich; **14.** Venetiae/Venice.

128. Break the spell: 1. Libya (Libra); **2.** China (chin); **3.** Mali (MMLI); **4.** Samoa (samosa); **5.** Oman (woman); **6.** Cyprus (Cyrus); **7.** Cameroon (Cameron); **8.** Tonga (tango); **9.** France (prance); **10.** Cuba (scuba); **11.** Benin (Lenin); **12.** Kenya (Kanye); **13.** Spain (spawn); **14.** Laos (Lagos); **15.** Liberia (Siberia); **16.** Bolivia (Olivia); **17.** Iran/Iraq; **18.** Gambia/Zambia.

129. In another world: 1. Land of Oz; **2.** Discworld; **3.** Jonathan Swift (in *Gulliver's Travels*); **4.** *Game of Thrones*; **5.** Bedrock; **6.** Narnia (it takes its name from the Umbrian town of Narni, or Narnia in Latin); **7.** Azeroth; **8.** Middle-earth; **9.** Finland; **10.** France; **11.** Lewis Carroll (real name Charles Dodgson); **12.** Springfield; **13.** Porterhouse (in *Porterhouse Blue*); **14.** *The Elder Scrolls*; **15.** Hundred Acre Wood; **16.** Asgard; **17.** Dinotopia; **18.** *The Archers*; **19.** Neverland; **20.** *Thomas the Tank Engine & Friends* (based on *The Railway Series* books).

130. Bitten by the travel bug: *Across:* **1.** haggis; **4.** skiing; **9A & 31A.** tonic water; **10.** origami; **11A & 12A.** happy feeling; **13.** red meat; **15.** panda; **17.** arnut; **18.** ensigns; **20.** make headway; **24.** takeout; **25.** taiga; **28.** needled; **29.** lobster; **33.** botanic;

34. Nauru; **35.** Arnhem; **36A & 5D.** pocket knife. *Down:* **1.** hit the road; **2.** genip; **3.** itchy feet; **6.** Iranian; **7D & 26A.** going Dutch; **8.** go off the beaten track; **14.** Denmark; **15.** posed; **16.** apse; **19.** gharial; **21.** epoch; **22.** stud; **23.** wanderlust; **25.** tae kwon do; **27.** Tibetan; **29.** Libya; **30.** tenge; **32.** trunk.